THE FUN FOOD
BOOK

THE FUN FOOD
BOOK

Anne Ager

CONTENTS

First published in 1983 by Octopus Books Limited
59 Grosvenor Street, London W1

Second impression, 1984

© 1983 Hennerwood Publications Limited

ISBN 0 86273 069 4

Printed in England by Severn Valley Press

INTRODUCTION

We all need to eat, but do not let us take it too seriously. Essentially, food should be fun – fun to prepare, and fun to eat. I can remember as a child, when I was just big enough to see over the top of the kitchen table, being given remnants of pastry to play with – they started off pale yellow in colour and ended up grey! No matter, if children are involved at an early age, their interest in food and cooking grows.

As a nation, we still have a lot to learn about the art of eating and the preparation of everyday meals. Invariably, the children expect to come in from school, drop their satchels, and somehow tea will magically appear. Occasionally husbands are just as bad, thinking that if they hide behind their newspaper long enough, dinner will be on the table. On the continent, the preparation of day-to-day meals is very much a family affair, each person doing their own little bit to help.

The idea of this book is to add a little extra sparkle and imagination to everyday eating, involving other members of the family and guests where possible. Although some of the recipes are out of the ordinary, all of them are geared to family eating and entertaining – imaginative without being too sophisticated.

Great Outdoors

The Great Outdoors includes food ideas for family picnics and barbecues in the garden. There are many appropriate 'portable' foods to choose from. Remember that fresh air tends to increase appetites, so make sure that you provide generous quantities of everything.

Table-Top Cooking

Whether for family eating or entertaining, cooking at the table is great fun. Guests enjoy cooking or par-preparing food for themselves when being entertained, hence the popularity of the fondue. A fondue-type meal can be a perfect choice for a family occasion, too. For fondue-style dishes, where the food is actually cooked in oil, you need a deep-sided pot with an under burner; for cheese and sauce fondues, a solid based fondue pot or casserole that will fit securely over a burner; and for the other top-of-the-table dishes, either an electric frying pan, chafing dish, or an attractive frying pan with an adjustable burner underneath. The symbol (T) in the method indicates at what point you should bring the fondue pot, frying pan or chafing dish to the table and do the cooking there, having done all the preparation, chopping and slicing, etc, in the kitchen.

Food on a Skewer

Food on a skewer is another novel way of presenting a meal for family or friends. Many foods, such as good quality steak and fillet of veal, benefit from quick cooking. When they are cut into small pieces and threaded on to skewers they cook quickly on the outside, but are still succulent and moist in the centre. Fish and fruit kebabs make appetizing dishes, too.

Skewers come in a variety of sizes, but a 27 cm (11 inch) skewer is the one most commonly used. This is the size skewer that has been used in most of the recipes in the book; if a particularly small size skewer is required, then this is specified. You can, of course, use a larger skewer, as long as you make sure that the ingredients are positioned in such a way that they will all fit under the source of heat from the grill.

Food that is threaded on to a skewer should not be packed too tightly, otherwise it affects the evenness of cooking and the overall cooking time; the skewered ingredients should touch, without being squashed together.

Grills vary so very much from one to another that it is difficult to give general advice. If your grill is prone to over-heating or getting very hot, then use a moderate setting; otherwise set the grill to full heat. You can always turn the heat down if the food shows signs of over-cooking. Ideally a kebab should cook about 10 cm (4 inches) away from the source of the heat; this ensures thorough cooking, without the food becoming too charred. If your grill is much deeper than this, then raise the food on a baking tin or something of a convenient size that is ovenproof. Alternatively, you can cook kebabs on a barbecue, as shown here. Remember that food usually cooks faster on a barbecue, so reduce the cooking time slightly and watch the food carefully in case it burns.

Special Sandwiches

Of course, sandwiches are 'portable' foods, too; but did you know that sandwiches come in many different guises, from the simple two-layered variety with a mere scraping of filling, to the American-style multi-layered sandwiches, laden with a variety of ingredients. This chapter provides a selection of rather special sandwiches, giving ideas for cocktail sandwiches, toasted sandwiches, party sandwiches, and those that are suitable for family suppers.

Sandwich toasters have become increasingly popular, and they are excellent for preparing a quick, hot snack. The last 5 recipes in this chapter are for toasted sandwiches, using a conventional grill for toasting. If you are using an electric sandwich toaster, reduce the amount of filling slightly, so that it comes well within the edges of the bread. There should be sufficient to give the sandwich a moist and tasty texture, but it should not ooze out between the two slices of bread. Do check the manufacturer's instructions carefully, as different models vary from one to another. Sandwiches toasted by this method tend to cook more quickly and also more evenly than if cooked under a grill.

All Wrapped Up

The other fun way of cooking is explained in this chapter. There is nothing new about parcel cooking – people have been cooking food in foil parcels ever since cooking foil was first introduced, and in the Middle East they have cooked food wrapped in leaves for thousands of years. However, you can be highly original in the wrapping that you use, and in choosing what goes inside. There are a few 'en croûte' recipes, using shortcrust and puff pastries; 'cooking' spaghetti in a greaseproof paper bag, so that it puffs up like a balloon and turns crisp; and some leaf recipes – cooking food in spinach and cabbage leaves.

Family Treats

This chapter contains unusual and colourful food ideas, for the whole family. Some would make ideal presents to give at Christmas or for birthdays. Many of the recipes are simple enough for children to make themselves, just as long as they have a little watchful supervision from a grown-up.

THE GREAT OUTDOORS

BARBECUE BITES

Serves 6
2 firm avocado pears, halved, stoned and peeled
juice of 2 lemons
¼ teaspoon ground ginger
salt
freshly ground black pepper
18 rashers streaky bacon

Preparation time: 15-20 minutes
Cooking time: 2-3 minutes

These small skewers of bacon and avocado make a perfect 'before the barbecue' snack, while everyone is waiting impatiently for the steaks, chops, etc, to cook.

1. Cut each avocado half into 9 even-sized cubes (it does not matter if they are not all quite the same shape). Toss the cubed avocado in the lemon juice, mixed with the ground ginger, salt and pepper.
2. Stretch the bacon rashers and cut each rasher in half crosswise. Roll up each cube of avocado in a piece of bacon. Thread on to 6 fine kebab skewers.
3. Place on the preheated barbecue grill and cook for 2-3 minutes.

BARBECUED SPARE-RIBS

1.75 kg (4 lb) pork spare-ribs (see below)
Baste:
6 tablespoons soy sauce
4 tablespoons oil
3 garlic cloves, peeled and crushed
1 small piece fresh ginger root or ¼ teaspoon dried ginger
grated rind of 1 lemon
few drops of Tabasco sauce
½ teaspoon ground cinnamon
salt
freshly ground black pepper
4 tablespoons clear honey

Preparation time: 5-10 minutes
Cooking time: 35-40 minutes (for separated ribs)

ARABIAN ORANGE SALAD

4 thin-skinned oranges, peeled
1 medium onion, peeled and cut into thin rings
50 g (2 oz) stoned black olives, sliced
Dressing:
6 tablespoons olive oil
juice of ½ lemon
1 tablespoon chopped fresh mint
1 tablespoon chopped pine kernels or blanched almonds
1 tablespoon chopped raisins
salt
freshly ground black pepper

Preparation time: 15-20 minutes, plus chilling

1. Remove all the pith from the oranges. Cut the flesh into thin slices, discarding any pips. Arrange the orange slices in a shallow dish with the onion rings and olives.
2. For the dressing, mix the oil, lemon juice, mint, nuts, raisins, and salt and pepper to taste, together. Spoon evenly over the orange slices. Cover and chill for one hour to allow the flavours to mingle.
3. To take on a picnic, pack the salad in a shallow polythene container, fitted with a lid.

There is not very much meat on spare-ribs, and, if they are to be eaten as a main course, you need to allow about 450 g (1 lb) per person. If the grill on the barbecue is widely spaced, leave the ribs unseparated, remembering that they will take longer to cook. Otherwise, separate the ribs, trimming off any jagged edges.

1. Prepare the spare-ribs as above.
2. For the baste, mix the soy sauce with the oil. Add the garlic and ginger, pressed through a garlic crusher, with lemon rind, Tabasco, cinnamon, salt and pepper.
3. Place the spare-ribs on the preheated barbecue grill, bone side downwards, and brush with the baste. Cook for about 10 minutes. Turn the ribs over, brush with more baste and cook for a further 15 minutes.
4. Turn the ribs once again and brush with the baste and honey. Cook for another 10-15 minutes.

FROM THE FRONT: Arabian orange salad; Barbecue bites; Barbecued spare-ribs

CHILLED CHICKEN PAPRIKA

1.5 kg (3 lb) cooked chicken, skinned
300 ml (½ pint) mayonnaise
150 ml (¼ pint) soured cream
1 tablespoon paprika
2 tablespoons tomato purée
½ teaspoon caster sugar
4 large tomatoes, skinned, seeded and chopped
salt
freshly ground black pepper
Pasta salad:
175 g (6 oz) pasta wheels or shells
1 small onion, peeled and finely chopped
6 tablespoons oil and vinegar dressing
2 tablespoons chopped fresh parsley

**Preparation time: 40-45 minutes, plus chilling
Cooking time: 8 minutes**

This recipe allows for about 4 generous servings; if you wish to make it go further, thin the sauce with a little milk or single cream, add 3 halved hard-boiled eggs and you should have sufficient to serve 6. For the salad, cook 225 g (8 oz) pasta.

1. Remove the chicken flesh and cut into neat bite-size pieces, putting the bones to one side. (Use the carcass and bones for making stock.)
2. Mix the mayonnaise with the soured cream, paprika, tomato purée, sugar, chopped tomatoes, and salt and pepper to taste. Stir in the chicken so that each piece is evenly coated in the sauce. Cover and chill for 2-3 hours.
3. For the Pasta salad, place the pasta wheels or shells in a saucepan of rapidly boiling salted water and cook for about 8 minutes until just tender. Drain the cooked pasta thoroughly.
4. Stir in the chopped onion and sufficient oil and vinegar dressing to moisten, while the pasta is still warm. Leave on one side until cool. Stir in the chopped parsley, and a little extra dressing if the pasta has already absorbed a great deal.
5. To take on a picnic, pack the chicken and salad in separate polythene containers, fitted with lids.

FROM THE LEFT: Pasta salad; Chilled chicken paprika; Cheese and watercress flan

CHEESE AND WATERCRESS FLAN

Serves 4-6
225 g (8 oz) prepared shortcrust pastry
Filling:
1 bunch watercress, about 50 g (2 oz), washed and shaken
   dry
175 g (6 oz) full fat soft cheese
4 tablespoons soured cream
2 eggs, separated
salt
freshly ground black pepper
2 tablespoons chicken stock or water
2 teaspoons powdered gelatine
4 spring onions, trimmed and finely chopped
To garnish:
3 tablespoons soured cream
coarsely chopped watercress

Preparation time: 55 minutes, plus chilling
Cooking time: 25-30 minutes
Oven: 190°C, 375°F, Gas Mark 5

The pastry case needs to be quite deep for the above quantity of filling. If you do not have a deep-sided flan tin, 20 cm (8 inches) in diameter, then use a slightly larger diameter flan tin.

1. Roll out the pastry and use to line a 20 cm (8 inch) fluted loose-bottomed flan tin. Line with a piece of greaseproof paper and a layer of baking beans. Place in a preheated oven and bake 'blind' for 15 minutes. Remove the paper and beans, return to the oven and continue cooking the pastry case for a further 10-15 minutes until the pastry is lightly golden. Remove from the oven and allow to cool, in its tin, on a wire tray.
2. Remove the base stalks and any discoloured leaves from the watercress. Chop quite finely. Beat the cheese with the soured cream, egg yolks, and salt and pepper to taste.
3. Place the chicken stock and gelatine into a small bowl. Stand in a pan of hot water and stir until the gelatine has dissolved. Beat the gelatine into the cheese mixture. Leave on one side until the mixture is on the point of setting.
4. Whisk the egg whites until stiff. Fold lightly but thoroughly into the cheese mixture, together with the chopped watercress and spring onions.
5. Spoon the mixture into the pastry case, smoothing the surface level. Chill until set. Spread the extra soured cream over the surface of the flan and sprinkle with the chopped watercress.
6. To take on a picnic, over-wrap the flan, still in its tin, with cling film or foil.

SWEDISH MEAT CAKES

3 slices white bread (from a large sliced loaf), crusts
   removed
150 ml (¼ pint) soda water
225 g (8 oz) minced veal
225 g (8 oz) minced pork
50 g (2 oz) ham, finely chopped
1 teaspoon juniper berries, crushed
2 egg yolks
salt
freshly ground black pepper
oil, for brushing
To serve:
4 large slices rye bread, spread with unsalted butter
1 medium onion, peeled and cut into thin rings
2 dill cucumbers, cut into fingers
2 tablespoons capers
150 ml (¼ pint) soured cream

Preparation time: 30 minutes, plus standing and chilling
Cooking time: 8 minutes

1. Break the bread into rough pieces and put into a shallow dish with the soda water. Leave to stand for 20 minutes.
2. Mix the minced and chopped meats with the juniper berries, egg yolks, and salt and pepper to taste. Add the moistened bread. Beat or work the mixture with the hands until smooth. Form into 4 burger shapes or meat cakes. Chill for 30 minutes.
3. Brush the meat cakes with oil. Place on the preheated barbecue grill and cook for 4 minutes. Turn the meat cakes over, brush with a little extra oil and cook for a further 4 minutes.
4. Place a slice of rye bread on each serving plate. Place a hot meat cake on each slice of rye bread and garnish with a few onion rings, a few fingers of dill cucumber and a small spoonful of capers. Add a swirl of soured cream to each plate.

Making meat cakes
The Scandinavians are masters at making meatballs and meat cakes; they combine a variety of different minced meats, and season the mixture subtly with spices and seasonings such as juniper berries, dill seed, ground allspice, etc. One secret is the addition of soda water to the basic mixture; it lightens the texture considerably. They also like meatball-style dishes slightly underdone or 'pink'; hence the reason in this recipe for using slices of bread as 'cushions' for the meat cakes – the bread absorbs the delicious meat juices.

MAPLE CHICKEN WITH ORANGE AND WATERCRESS

4 chicken legs
Marinade:
200 ml (⅓ pint) unsweetened orange juice
1 medium onion, peeled and thinly sliced
1 garlic clove, peeled and crushed
salt
freshly ground black pepper
freshly grated nutmeg
4 tablespoons maple syrup
Orange and watercress salad:
4 thin-skinned oranges
1 bunch watercress, washed and shaken dry
1 small onion, peeled and finely chopped
4 tablespoons olive oil
2 tablespoons chopped fresh chives or parsley
salt
freshly ground black pepper

Preparation time: 30 minutes, plus chilling overnight
Cooking time: 30-35 minutes

Maple syrup gives the chicken a characteristic flavour, but you can use a good quality clear honey instead. The flavour of the chicken is enhanced by marinating overnight.

1. Pierce the chicken legs at regular intervals with a fine skewer and put them into a shallow dish. Add the orange juice, sliced onion, garlic, salt, pepper and nutmeg to taste. Cover the dish and chill for 8 hours or overnight.
2. Remove the chicken joints from their marinade, allowing the excess to drip off. Place on the preheated barbecue grill, flesh side down, and cook for 15 minutes. Turn the chicken joints over, brush with maple syrup and cook for a further 15-20 minutes until tender. Test the chicken by piercing the joints in the thickest part with a fine skewer – if the juices run clear, not pink, the chicken is cooked. Serve the chicken portions hot with the salad.
3. For the Orange and watercress salad, grate the rind and squeeze the juice from 1 orange. Remove all the pith and peel from the remaining 3 oranges. Divide into segments.
4. Snip the watercress into sprigs. Put the orange segments and watercress into a shallow serving dish and sprinkle with the chopped onion. Mix the orange juice and rind with the olive oil, chives, and salt and pepper to taste. Spoon the dressing over the salad.

TOP: Swedish meat cakes. BOTTOM: Maple chicken with orange and watercress

GUINNESS MEAT LOAF

Serves 6
100 g (4 oz) fresh white breadcrumbs
200 ml (⅓ pint) Guinness
350 g (12 oz) minced beef
350 g (12 oz) minced pork
1 tablespoon chopped fresh rosemary
1 egg, beaten
salt
freshly ground black pepper
freshly grated nutmeg
1 small onion, peeled and finely chopped
100 g (4 oz) Edam cheese, cut into small cubes

Preparation time: 15 minutes, plus soaking and cooling
Cooking time: 1½ hours
Oven: 180°C, 350°F, Gas Mark 4

This meat loaf has a rich, slightly bitter flavour from the Guinness. A sweet stout or a medium dry cider could be substituted if preferred.

1. Place the breadcrumbs in a bowl with the Guinness. Cover and leave on one side for 30 minutes.
2. Mix the minced meats in a bowl with the rosemary, beaten egg, salt, pepper and nutmeg to taste, and the onion. Add the Guinness-soaked breadcrumbs and mix thoroughly together.
3. Grease and line a 1 kg (2 lb) loaf tin. Stir the cheese cubes into the meat mixture. Spoon into the prepared loaf tin, smoothing the surface level. Cover with a piece of greased foil.
4. Place in a preheated oven and cook for 1½ hours. Remove the cooked meat loaf from the oven. Peel back the foil and carefully tip off any excess juices from the tin. Leave until quite cold before slicing.
5. To take on a picnic, over-wrap the loaf in foil, to keep it moist. Serve with radishes and spring onions.

TOMATO VICHYSSOISE

Serves 6
40 g (1½ oz) butter
1 medium onion, peeled and finely chopped
350 g (12 oz) potatoes, peeled and roughly chopped
350 g (12 oz) tomatoes, roughly chopped
1 garlic clove, peeled and crushed
1 tablespoon tomato purée
1 tablespoon chopped fresh basil (optional)
450 ml (¾ pint) chicken stock
450 ml (¾ pint) milk
salt
freshly ground black pepper
150 ml (¼ pint) double cream
chopped fresh parsley or basil, to garnish

Preparation time: 15 minutes, plus chilling
Cooking time: 30-35 minutes

This soup makes a delicious starter for a barbecue meal; alternatively the chilled soup can be packed into a flask to take on a picnic.

1. Heat the butter in a pan, add the onion and fry gently for 3 minutes. Add the potatoes, tomatoes, garlic, tomato purée, basil, stock, milk, and salt and pepper to taste. Bring to the boil and simmer for 25-30 minutes.
2. Either sieve the soup, or blend in the liquidizer until smooth. Allow to cool, then stir in the cream.
3. Chill the soup thoroughly. Garnish with the chopped parsley or basil and serve with crusty bread.

STRAWBERRY CHEESE MOUSSE

Serves 6
350 g (12 oz) Ricotta or curd cheese
75 g (3 oz) caster sugar
few drops of vanilla essence
2 eggs, separated
300 ml (½ pint) double cream
2 tablespoons water
15 g (½ oz) powdered gelatine
225 g (8 oz) strawberries, hulled and chopped
To decorate:
whipped cream
8 whole strawberries

Preparation time: 30 minutes, plus chilling

1. Grease a 1.5 litre (2½ pint) heart-shaped mould. (Any other shaped mould can be used, as long as it is the same capacity.)
2. Beat the cheese with the caster sugar, vanilla essence, egg yolks and double cream until smooth.
3. Put the water and gelatine into a small bowl. Stand inside a saucepan of hot water and stir until the gelatine has dissolved. Stir into the cheese mixture.
4. Whisk the egg whites until stiff, as soon as the mixture starts to set, and fold lightly but thoroughly into the mixture, together with the chopped strawberries.
5. Pour into the prepared mould and chill until set.
6. Unmould carefully on to a flat serving dish and decorate with whipped cream and strawberries.

LEFT: Guinness meat loaf. RIGHT: Strawberry cheese mousse

POTTED CHEESE

Makes about 450 g (1 lb)
350 g (12 oz) Stilton cheese, crumbled
100 g (4 oz) unsalted butter, softened
freshly ground black pepper
pinch of grated nutmeg
3 tablespoons port
2 tablespoons blanched almonds, chopped and toasted
melted or clarified butter (see below)
few whole toasted almonds

Preparation time: 20-25 minutes, plus chilling

This is a good old-fashioned way of making cheese last longer.

To make clarified butter, heat the butter slowly in a pan until melted and frothy. Chill in the refrigerator for a few hours until a thick layer of clarified butter sets on the top – the sediment will be left underneath. Scoop off the surface set butter and melt in a saucepan – this melted butter will be quite clear. The remaining butter and sediment can be used for frying food when a 'clear' butter is not required.

1. Pound the crumbled cheese with the softened butter until thoroughly blended.
2. Add pepper and nutmeg to taste, and beat in the port and almonds.
3. Press the cheese mixture into small pots. Cover with a thin layer of melted or clarified butter.
4. Once the butter starts to set, press a whole toasted almond into the top of each one. Store in a cool place.

BROWN SUGAR AND CHESTNUT MERINGUES

Makes 10

3 egg whites
175 g (6 oz) golden granulated sugar
200 ml (⅓ pint) double cream
4 tablespoons sweetened chestnut spread (crème de
   marrons)

Preparation time: 25-30 minutes
Cooking time: 2 hours
Oven: 120°C, 250°F, Gas Mark ½

Brown sugar adds a delicious caramel flavour to a
basic meringue mixture.

1. Lightly grease 2 baking sheets and line with non-
stick silicone paper.
2. Whisk the egg whites until stiff. Add half the sugar
and whisk once again until stiff.
3. Fold in the remaining sugar, lightly but thoroughly.
4. Using a large piping bag and a large star nozzle,
pipe 20 large rosettes on to the prepared baking sheets.
5. Bake in the oven for 2 hours until dry. Allow to cool
before removing from the baking sheets.
6. Whip the cream until thick and fold in the chestnut
purée.
7. Sandwich the meringue shells together in pairs
with the chestnut cream filling.

FROM THE LEFT: Rich cherry and almond dessert; Brown sugar and
chestnut meringues; No-bake Brazil cake

NO-BAKE BRAZIL CAKE

Makes one 1 kg (2 lb) cake
225 g (8 oz) digestive biscuits, coarsely crumbled
175 g (6 oz) candied peel, chopped
175 g (6 oz) glacé cherries, chopped
100 g (4 oz) raisins
100 g (4 oz) Brazil nuts, chopped
1 teaspoon ground mixed spice
75 g (3 oz) marshmallows, chopped
3 tablespoons sherry
3 tablespoons black treacle
100 g (4 oz) plain chocolate, broken into small pieces

Preparation time: 20 minutes, plus chilling
Cooking time: 5 minutes

1. Lightly grease a 1 kg (2 lb) loaf tin and line with greased greaseproof paper.
2. Mix the crumbled biscuits with the peel, cherries, raisins, nuts and mixed spice.
3. Place the marshmallows, sherry, black treacle and chocolate in a bowl. Stand the bowl over a saucepan of gently simmering water and stir until all the ingredients have melted.
4. Stir the melted ingredients into the biscuit and fruit mixture, and mix thoroughly together.
5. Pour into the prepared loaf tin and spread the surface level. Cover with a piece of greased greaseproof paper.
6. Chill until the cake is quite firm. Unmould from the tin and over-wrap the cake in foil. Keep in a cool place.

RICH CHERRY AND ALMOND DESSERT

Makes one 25 cm (10 inch) cake
1 × 450 g (1 lb) jar morello cherries
6 eggs, separated
150 g (5 oz) caster sugar
½ teaspoon almond essence
150 g (5 oz) plain flour
1 tablespoon cocoa powder
3 tablespoons olive oil
Topping:
4 tablespoons redcurrant jelly
175 g (6 oz) plain chocolate, melted
4 tablespoons flaked almonds

Preparation time: 35-40 minutes
Cooking time: 55 minutes
Oven: 180°C, 350°F, Gas Mark 4

Layered fruit cakes
Although this cake has a moist texture, which keeps fairly well, it does contain bottled morello cherries, which are perishable; it is therefore advisable to keep it for no longer than 4-5 days, stored well wrapped and in a cool place. Other fruits can be baked between the layers of cake mixture in the same way – you might like to try a variation using sections of well drained canned pear, thin chunks of pineapple or mandarin oranges. (Do make sure that all canned fruits are drained very thoroughly.) The redcurrant, chocolate and almond topping is suitable to use with most fruits.

This cake has a really moist texture, so don't be misled into thinking you haven't cooked it sufficiently.
If the occasion is really special, sprinkle 3-4 tablespoons brandy over the cooked cake, instead of the cherry and redcurrant liquid.

1. Strain the cherries, reserving the juice, and drain the cherries very thoroughly on paper towels. Grease and line a 25 cm (10 inch) round loose-bottomed cake tin.
2. Whisk the egg whites until stiff, then whisk in half the caster sugar. Fold in the remaining sugar.
3. Beat the egg yolks with the almond essence and fold into the whisked egg whites. Fold in the sifted flour and cocoa, then the olive oil. Spoon just under half the mixture into the prepared tin, smoothing the surface level.
4. Place in a preheated oven and bake for 10 minutes. Arrange the drained cherries over the part-cooked sponge layer, then cover with the rest of the sponge mixture, smoothing it level. Return to the oven and continue cooking the cake for a further 40 minutes.
5. Meanwhile measure 6 tablespoons of the cherry juice into a small pan. Add the redcurrant jelly and stir over a gentle heat until dissolved. Simmer for 2-3 minutes.
6. Ease the sides of the cake away from the tin. Lift the cake carefully out of the tin and remove the tin base. Stand the cake on a wire tray over a tray – this will catch any drips of juice.
7. Pierce the cake at regular intervals with a fine skewer. Spoon the cherry and redcurrant liquid evenly over the cake. Leave until quite cold.
8. Spread the melted chocolate over the top and sides of the cake. Sprinkle the edge with flaked almonds and press flaked almonds gently on to the sides with a round-bladed knife. Wrap the cake well to keep it moist.

TABLE-TOP COOKING

STEAKS WITH GREEN PEPPERCORN SAUCE

25 g (1 oz) butter
2 tablespoons oil
4 fillet steaks, about 1 cm (½ inch) thick, and about 175 g (6 oz) each
150 ml (¼ pint) double cream
1 garlic clove, peeled and crushed
2 teaspoons green peppercorns
salt
1 tablespoon chopped fresh parsley

Preparation time: about 5 minutes
Cooking time: 4-5 minutes

The cooking time can be increased depending on how well done you like your steaks.

1. Ⓣ Heat the butter and oil in an electric frying pan or decorative frying pan over an adjustable burner.
2. Add the fillet steaks and fry for about 1 minute on each side, depending on personal preference.
3. Remove the steaks to a plate and keep warm.
4. Add the cream, garlic, peppercorns, salt and parsley to the fat remaining in the pan.
5. Heat briskly for 1 minute and then add the steaks to the sauce in the pan. Heat together for 1 minute.

FONDUE BOURGUIGNONNE

500 g (1¼ lb) fillet steak
parsley sprigs, watercress or lettuce, to garnish
groundnut oil, for deep frying
To serve:
accompanying sauces (see below)
French bread
green salad

Preparation time: about 10 minutes, plus making sauces
Cooking time: 4-5 minutes

1. Cut the fillet steak into 1 cm (½ inch) cubes. Arrange on 4 individual plates, garnishing the meat with parsley, watercress or lettuce if liked.
2. Add sufficient groundnut oil almost to half fill the fondue pot. Heat the oil on the top of the cooker to 190°C (375°F), or until a cube of bread browns in 30 seconds, and then transfer to the fondue burner Ⓣ.
3. Provide each person with a plate of cubed steak; a fondue fork for spearing and cooking the steak; and a knife and fork for eating the meat, for those who prefer to be more conventional.
4. Each person can then cook their steak in the hot oil – the length of time depends on how rare or well done each person prefers their meat.
5. Provide a selection of sauces for dipping the cooked steak into, a basket of hot French bread and a bowl of green salad.

Sauces for Fondue Bourguignonne:
Horseradish sauce: Mix together 1 tablespoon grated fresh horseradish, juice of ½ lemon, pinch of caster sugar, 150 ml (¼ pint) soured cream, and salt and pepper to taste.
Mustard sauce: Mix together 1 small onion, peeled and finely chopped, 150 ml (¼ pint) mayonnaise, 1 tablespoon French mustard, ½ teaspoon cayenne pepper, and salt to taste.
Salsa verde (Green sauce): Blend together in the liquidizer 2 tablespoons capers, 4 gherkins, 2 garlic cloves, peeled, 4 tablespoons olive oil, 4 tablespoons white wine vinegar, 2 tablespoons roughly chopped fresh parsley, pinch of caster sugar, and salt and pepper to taste.
Cold curry sauce: Mix 150 ml (¼ pint) double cream with 1 tablespoon mild curry powder, finely grated rind of ½ lemon, 1 tablespoon raisins, and salt to taste.

LEFT: Steaks with green peppercorn sauce. RIGHT: Fondue Bourguignonne

SEAFOOD AND WHITE WINE FONDUE

350 g (12 oz) white fish fillet
100 g (4 oz) self-raising flour
generous pinch of salt
1 egg
150 ml (¼ pint) water
oil, for deep frying
Fondue:
65 g (2½ oz) butter
65 g (2½ oz) plain flour
300 ml (½ pint) chicken stock
450 ml (¾ pint) dry white wine
salt
freshly ground black pepper
150 ml (¼ pint) double cream
3 egg yolks
To dip:
175 g (6 oz) large peeled prawns
225 g (8 oz) shelled mussels

Preparation time: 25 minutes
Cooking time: 7-8 minutes

Use a wide fondue pot for this dish, similar to that used for making a cheese fondue.

1. Cut the fish fillet into 2 cm (¾ inch) cubes.
2. Sift the self-raising flour and salt into a bowl. Add the egg and a little of the water and beat until smooth. Beat in the remaining water.
3. Dip each piece of fish into the batter to give an even coating. Fill a deep pan one third full with oil and heat to 190°C (375°F), or until a cube of bread browns in 30 seconds. Lower the fish into the hot oil and fry for about 3 minutes until crisp and golden. Drain on paper towels.
4. The crispy fish pieces can be prepared up to an hour in advance and then crisped up in a moderately hot oven.
5. For the fondue, melt the butter in a pan and stir in the flour. Cook for 1 minute, stirring.
6. Gradually stir in the chicken stock and wine, whisking until the sauce is smooth. Add salt and pepper to taste.
7. Ⓣ Transfer the wine sauce to the fondue pot and place over the burner.
8. Beat the cream with the egg yolks and gradually stir into the hot wine sauce – make sure that the fondue does not boil at this stage.
9. Divide the crispy fish pieces, prawns and mussels on to 4 individual plates, and use to dip. Accompany with chunks of hot French bread.

BEER AND GOUDA FONDUE

1 garlic clove, peeled and bruised
300 ml (½ pint) brown ale
400 g (14 oz) Gouda cheese, grated
1 tablespoon flour
salt
freshly ground black pepper
1 teaspoon caraway seeds
2.5 cm (1 inch) cubes of bread, to dip

Preparation time: about 5 minutes
Cooking time: 10 minutes

LEFT: Beer and Gouda fondue. RIGHT: Seafood and white wine fondue

This is quite a thick cheese fondue. It is important not to heat the cheese too briskly.

1. Rub the inside of the fondue pot with the garlic clove and then discard it.
2. Put the brown ale into the fondue pot. Heat on top of the cooker until the beer just reaches boiling point.
3. Mix the grated cheese with the flour and add to the hot brown ale, whisking or stirring until smooth.
4. Add salt and pepper to taste and the caraway seeds.
5. (T) Transfer the fondue to the burner. Serve with the cubes of bread to dip.

COTTAGE CHEESE AND CHIVE FONDUE

225 g (8 oz) natural cottage cheese
225 g (8 oz) Emmenthal cheese, grated
1½ tablespoons plain flour
300 ml (½ pint) dry cider or white wine
1 tablespoon Worcestershire sauce
2 teaspoons French mustard
2 tablespoons chopped fresh chives
salt
freshly ground black pepper
cubes of bread, to dip

Preparation time: 5 minutes
Cooking time: 10 minutes

1. Sieve the cottage cheese and mix with the grated cheese and flour.
2. Put the cider or wine into the fondue pot. Heat on top of the cooker until the cider just reaches boiling point.
3. Add the cheese and flour mixture, whisking or stirring until smooth.
4. Add the Worcestershire sauce, mustard, chives and salt and pepper to taste.
5. (T) Transfer the fondue to the burner. Serve with cubes of bread, or slices of toasted French bread to dip.

CRAB FONDUE

1 garlic clove, peeled and bruised
300 ml (½ pint) dry white wine
275 g (10 oz) mild Cheddar cheese, grated
1 tablespoon flour
salt
freshly ground black pepper
175 g (6 oz) white crab meat, flaked
puff pastry crescents or cheese straws, to dip

Preparation time: 5 minutes
Cooking time: 10 minutes

1. Rub the inside of the fondue pot with the garlic, then discard it.
2. Put the white wine into the fondue pot. Heat on top of the cooker until the wine just reaches boiling point.
3. Mix the grated cheese with the flour and add to the hot wine, whisking or stirring until smooth.
4. Add salt and pepper to taste and the crab meat.
5. (T) Transfer the fondue to the burner, and serve with crescents of puff pastry or cheese straws to dip.

CHINESE FONDUE

1 litre (1¾ pints) chicken stock, either homemade or made
　from 2 stock cubes and water
1 onion, peeled and thinly sliced
1 large carrot, peeled and sliced
1 stick celery, chopped
4 large mushrooms, sliced
3 slices fresh root ginger
To dip:
175 g (6 oz) tiny button mushrooms
1 heart Chinese cabbage, shredded
½ small cauliflower, divided into tiny florets
100 g (4 oz) mangetout peas or a handful of small spinach
　leaves
100 g (4 oz) peeled prawns
175 g (6 oz) boned chicken, cut into thin strips or slivers
175 g (6 oz) calves' liver, cut into thin strips or slivers
175 g (6 oz) fillet of beef, cut into thin strips or slivers
175 g (6 oz) pork fillet, cut into thin strips or slivers
To serve:
boiled rice or noodles
accompanying sauces (see below)

**Preparation time: about 45 minutes, plus making
sauces
Cooking time: 10 minutes for the stock; ½-1 minute
to dip each item**

Almost a complete chapter could be written on this
classic Chinese-style fondue – sometimes referred to as
a hotpot or firepot. Instead of using hot oil to cook
pieces of food in, or a hot cheese mixture in which to
dip pieces of food, a well-flavoured stock is used as the
fondue base.

An attractive array of foods is presented alongside
the 'stockpot', all cut into sufficiently small pieces so
that they cook quickly – whole peeled prawns; thin
strips of chicken, pork, veal, liver or lean tender beef;
small whole button mushrooms (or sliced dried
mushrooms, which have been soaked for 30 minutes);
strips of Chinese cabbage; tiny florets of cauliflower;
small spinach leaves; mangetout peas.

The stock base for the fondue has a better flavour if
pieces of vegetable are added to the stock right at the
beginning of cooking, and left in – sliced onion, strips
of pepper, carrot and celery, and sliced mushrooms.
Fresh root ginger is also added to give the stock its
characteristic flavour; the flavour actually improves as
the meal progresses. Special Chinese 'kettles' for preparing this meal can be bought from Chinese stores.
You can, however, use a small adjustable spirit burner
with an attractive saucepan or fondue pot placed on
top. Each person is given a pair of chopsticks and/or a
small metal ladle, for lowering the food into the hot
stock, and for retrieving it; a fork for eating with, if
chopsticks cannot be coped with; and a soup bowl and

spoon, for drinking the stock, once the cooking and
eating of the meat, fish and vegetables has finished.

The Chinese fondue is accompanied by small bowls
of rice or noodles, and 2 or more well-flavoured sauces
for dipping the cooked food into. Five sauces are given
here for you to choose from.

1. Put the stock into a saucepan with the onion, carrot,
celery, sliced mushrooms and ginger. Simmer gently
for 10 minutes.
2. Arrange the prepared mushrooms, cabbage, cauliflower, mangetout, prawns, chicken, liver, beef and
pork decoratively on a platter, grouping them accord-
ing to type.
3. ⓣ Transfer the stock to the Chinese kettle or fondue
pot, and place over the burner – it should be kept at a
steady heat during the meal.
4. Provide each person with a few bowls of different
flavoured sauces, so that they can dip the selected
pieces of food once they are cooked, and an accompanying bowl of hot boiled rice or noodles.

Sauces for Chinese fondue:
Soy and garlic sauce: Put 150 ml (¼ pint) soy sauce
into a pan with 3 garlic cloves, peeled and crushed or
finely chopped. Simmer for 1-2 minutes and serve
either warm or cold.
Plum sauce: You can buy this sauce ready prepared
from Chinese food shops and some delicatessens.
Alternatively, mix 6 tablespoons plum jam with 2
tablespoons vinegar and 2 tablespoons chopped man-
go chutney. Serve cold. (If the jam is chunky, sieve it.)
Green onion sauce: Mix 6 tablespoons olive oil with 3
spring onions, finely chopped, 1 garlic clove, peeled
and crushed, 1 tablespoon sesame seeds, and salt and
pepper to taste.
Lime and pepper sauce: Mix the juice of 2 freshly
squeezed limes with salt and pepper to taste, 1 red
pepper, cored, seeded and very finely chopped, 1
small onion, peeled and finely chopped and 3 tablespoons olive oil.
Fiery tomato sauce: Mix 4 tablespoons tomato purée
with ½ teaspoon chilli powder, 2 teaspoons soy sauce,
1 garlic clove, peeled and crushed, salt to taste, 1 teaspoon caster sugar and juice of 1 lemon.

1. Slicing the pork fillet thinly.

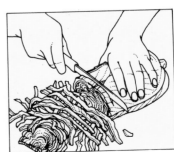

2. Shredding a Chinese cabbage
heart.

SPRING ROLLS

Serves 4-6
100 g (4 oz) plain flour
about 75 g (3 oz) cornflour
salt
1 egg
200 ml (⅓ pint) water
oil, for deep frying
Filling:
175 g (6 oz) cooked chicken, minced
1 tablespoon soy sauce
4 Chinese cabbage leaves, coarsely shredded
3 spring onions, trimmed and coarsely chopped
4 canned water chestnuts, finely chopped
freshly ground black pepper
Sweet and sour sauce:
4 tablespoons red wine vinegar
4 tablespoons brown sugar
300 ml (½ pint) chicken stock
1 tablespoon tomato purée
2 teaspoons soy sauce

Preparation time: 30-35 minutes
Cooking time: 17-18 minutes

Small Chinese-style pancakes are a perfect choice for cooking at the table – use a fondue pot (one that is used for meat fondue) one-third filled with oil.

1. Sift the flour, 50 g (2 oz) of the cornflour and ½ teaspoon salt into a bowl.
2. Make a well in the centre. Add the egg and a little of the water and beat to a paste. Gradually whisk in the remaining water.
3. For the filling, mix together the chicken, soy sauce, shredded cabbage, spring onions, water chestnuts, and salt and pepper to taste.
4. Mix 1 tablespoon of the remaining cornflour with a little water in a cup to give a smooth paste.
5. Brush a small omelette or pancake pan with a little oil. Add 1 tablespoon of the batter and tilt the pan to give a thin, even layer. Cook the pancake for about 1 minute on the underside only, and place on a greased tray.
6. Continue with the remaining batter until you have made 12-14 small pancakes, all cooked on one side only.
7. Lay the pancakes out, cooked surfaces uppermost. Divide the filling between the pancakes and spread a little of the cornflour paste around the outer edge of each pancake.
8. Roll up the pancakes, tucking the ends in firmly, sealing them with a little more cornflour paste if necessary. (The prepared pancakes can be chilled at this stage until needed.)

9. For the Sweet and sour sauce, put all the ingredients into a pan and bring to the boil. Mix the remaining 2 tablespoons cornflour with 3 tablespoons cold water and stir on the hot liquid. Return the sauce to the pan and stir over a moderate heat until smooth and thickened.
10. Ⓣ One third fill the fondue pot with oil and heat to 190°C (375°F), or until a cube of bread browns in 30 seconds.
11. Lower the pancakes carefully into the hot oil and deep fry for 2-3 minutes on each side until crisp and golden.
12. Provide each person with a plate covered with paper towels, and a small bowl of sauce.

LEFT: Spring rolls. RIGHT: Pan-fried trout with grapes

PAN-FRIED TROUT WITH GRAPES

8 trout fillets (i.e. 4 small trout, filleted)
50 g (2 oz) butter
1 small onion, peeled and finely chopped
grated rind of ½ lemon
6 tablespoons dry white vermouth
salt
freshly ground black pepper
2 tablespoons chopped fresh parsley
4 tablespoons double cream
100 g (4 oz) green grapes, skinned and seeded
1 tablespoon chopped fresh mint (when available)

Preparation time: 20 minutes
Cooking time: 10-15 minutes

1. Remove any loose bones that may have been left on the trout fillets.
2. Ⓣ Put the butter into an electric frying pan or decorative frying pan placed over an adjustable burner. Melt the butter over a moderate heat.
3. Add the trout fillets, skin side uppermost, and cook for 2-3 minutes. Turn the fillets over and cook for a further 2-3 minutes.
4. Remove the trout fillets to a heated plate.
5. Add the onion, lemon rind, vermouth, salt and pepper to taste, and the parsley to the pan. Cook briskly until reduced by half.
6. Stir in the cream and return the trout fillets to the pan. Add the grapes and cook for 1 minute, being careful not to let it come to the boil. Sprinkle with mint, if using.

VEAL GOUJONS WITH SPICY TOMATO SAUCE

750 g (1½ lb) veal fillet
lettuce leaves
parsley sprigs, to garnish
cooking or groundnut oil, for deep frying
Spicy tomato sauce:
150 ml (¼ pint) soured cream
3 tablespoons tomato purée
1 tablespoon Worcestershire sauce
1 tablespoon French mustard
1 garlic clove, peeled and crushed
salt
freshly ground black pepper

Preparation time: 15 minutes
Cooking time: 3 minutes

1. Cut the veal fillet into fingers about 5 mm (¼ inch) wide and 5 cm (2 inches) long. Arrange on 4 small individual plates, on a bed of lettuce and garnished with parsley.
2. Add sufficient oil to half fill the fondue pot. Heat the oil on top of the cooker to 190°C (375°F), or until a cube of bread browns in 30 seconds, and then transfer the pot to the fondue burner Ⓣ.
3. For the sauce, mix together the remaining ingredients.
4. The thin strips of veal will cook in the hot oil within 20-30 seconds. Serve with the Spicy tomato sauce, hot crusty bread and a green salad.

SAUTÉ SPICED LAMB

500 g (1¼ lb) lamb fillet
50 g (2 oz) butter
1 medium onion, peeled and finely chopped
1 garlic clove, peeled and crushed
½ teaspoon ground cinnamon
2 teaspoons cornflour
150 ml (¼ pint) chicken stock
150 ml (¼ pint) soured cream
1 tablespoon chopped fresh mint
salt
freshly ground black pepper

Preparation time: 5 minutes
Cooking time: about 15 minutes

VEAL ESCALOPES WITH SAGE

4 veal escalopes, about 100 g (4 oz) each, well beaten
25 g (1 oz) butter
2 tablespoons oil
1 small onion, peeled and finely chopped
1 tablespoon chopped fresh sage
50 g (2 oz) ham, cut into strips
75 g (3 oz) button mushrooms, sliced
salt
freshly ground black pepper
3 tablespoons brandy
4 tablespoons double cream
fresh sage leaves, to garnish

Preparation time: 10-15 minutes
Cooking time: 10-12 minutes

1. Cut the veal escalopes into small pieces, about 5 cm (2 inches) square.
2. Ⓣ Heat the butter and oil in an electric frying pan or decorative frying pan over an adjustable burner. Add the onion and fry gently.
3. Add the pieces of veal and fry gently on either side for 1-2 minutes until tender. Remove the veal to a plate and keep warm, covering tightly with foil.
4. Add the sage, ham and mushrooms to the fat remaining in the pan and fry quickly for 2 minutes.
5. Add salt and pepper to taste, the brandy and cream and bring just to the boil.
6. Return the veal to the pan and heat through in the sauce for 1 minute.
7. Garnish with fresh sage leaves, if liked.

1. Cut the lamb fillet into thin slices about 5 mm (¼ inch) thick.
2. Ⓣ Heat the butter either in an electric frying pan, or in a decorative frying pan over an adjustable burner.
3. Add the onion, garlic and cinnamon and fry gently until the onion softens.
4. Add the slices of lamb fillet and cook steadily, turning occasionally, until the lamb is coloured on all sides.
5. Blend the cornflour with the stock and soured cream and add to the pan.
6. Stir until the sauce thickens slightly. Add the mint and salt and pepper to taste, and simmer gently for 8-10 minutes, until the lamb is tender.
7. Serve hot with noodles or rice.

FROM THE FRONT: Sauté spiced lamb; Veal escalopes with sage

FLAMBÉED BANANAS

50 g (2 oz) butter
4 large bananas, peeled
4 tablespoons dark rum
2 tablespoons demerara sugar
To serve:
wedges of lime or lemon
whipped cream

Preparation time: about 5 minutes
Cooking time: 2-3 minutes

1. Ⓣ Put the butter into an electric frying pan or decorative frying pan over an adjustable burner. Heat gently until the butter melts.
2. Cut the bananas in half lengthways.
3. Add the bananas to the hot butter and cook for 1 minute, turning the bananas in the butter.
4. Heat a metal ladle and add the rum. Carefully set light to it and pour over the bananas.
5. As soon as the flames die down, sprinkle the bananas with the demerara sugar and baste with the butter and rum liquid.
6. Serve hot with wedges of lime or lemon and whipped cream.

CHERRY COMPÔTE

Serves 6
2 × 425 g (15 oz) cans black cherries
4 tablespoons soft brown sugar
finely grated rind of ½ orange
4 tablespoons Kirsch

Preparation time: 2-3 minutes
Cooking time: about 6 minutes

1. Drain the cherries, reserving the syrup or juice from the cans.
2. Ⓣ Put 200 ml (⅓ pint) of the cherry juice into an electric frying pan, or into a decorative pan over an adjustable burner, and heat gently.
3. Add the sugar and orange rind and stir until the sugar has dissolved. Cook over a gentle heat until the syrup has reduced slightly.
4. Add the cherries to the prepared syrup and heat through.
5. Heat a metal ladle and add the Kirsch. Carefully set light to the Kirsch and pour over the cherries.
6. As soon as the flames die down, serve hot with ice cream.

CHOCOLATE AND HONEY FONDUE

Serves 4-6
300 ml (½ pint) milk
1½ tablespoons cornflour
300 ml (½ pint) single cream
175 g (6 oz) plain chocolate, grated
4 tablespoons clear honey
finely grated rind of ½ orange
To dip:
cubes of madeira cake or plain sponge cake
pieces of crystallized ginger
marshmallows

Preparation time: about 15 minutes
Cooking time: 6 minutes

1. Mix 4 tablespoons of the milk with the cornflour to a smooth paste.
2. Put the remaining milk into a saucepan with the cream, chocolate, honey and orange rind.
3. Stir over a gentle heat until the chocolate has melted.
4. Stir the flavoured milk on to the cornflour paste, mixing well, and return the mixture to the pan.
5. Stir over a gentle heat until the fondue has thickened.
6. Ⓣ Pour into a fondue pot or casserole and stand over the burner – take care that the fondue does not stick to the pot and burn.
7. Serve with the madeira or sponge cake cubes, ginger and marshmallows to dip.

LEFT: Flambéed bananas. RIGHT: Chocolate and honey fondue

LEMON FONDUE

Serves 4-6

600 ml (1 pint) single cream
5 egg yolks
finely grated rind of 3 lemons
50 g (2 oz) caster sugar
To dip:
cubes of gingerbread and/or brandy snaps

Preparation time: about 5 minutes
Cooking time: about 15 minutes

1. Heat the cream in the top of a double saucepan until tepid, or use a heatproof bowl over a pan of simmering water.

2. Put the egg yolks, lemon rind and caster sugar into a bowl and whisk until thick and creamy.

3. Pour the tepid cream on to the egg yolk mixture and whisk in.

4. Return the lemon mixture to the top of the double saucepan and cook, stirring, until the fondue mixture will coat the back of a wooden spoon.

5. Ⓣ Transfer the fondue to an ovenproof bowl and place over a fondue pan of simmering water.

6. Serve with gingerbread cubes or brandy snaps.

PINEAPPLE WITH CARAMEL SAUCE

1 small fresh pineapple
6 tablespoons Kirsch or brandy
75 g (3 oz) butter
3 tablespoons soft brown sugar
grated rind and juice of 1 small orange
pouring or whipping cream, to serve

Preparation time: 25 minutes, plus chilling
Cooking time: 6-8 minutes

This pudding can be made with rings of canned pineapple, but it has a much better flavour if fresh pineapple is used. It is not necessary to remove the core of the pineapple, but can be done if preferred.

1. Remove the pine and stalk end from the pineapple. Cut off all the other peel, so that there are no coarse 'eyes' left on the pineapple.
2. Cut the pineapple into 8 even-sized slices.
3. Put the pineapple slices into a shallow dish and spoon over 4 tablespoons of the Kirsch or brandy. Cover and chill for 3-4 hours.
4. Drain the pineapple slices, reserving the liquid.
5. ⓉPut the butter into an electric frying pan or decorative frying pan over an adjustable burner. Heat gently until the butter melts.
6. Add the brown sugar and cook briskly for a few seconds until the mixture bubbles. Stir in the orange rind and juice.
7. Add the slices of pineapple to the caramel sauce, and stir over the heat for 2 minutes, then pour over the reserved liquid.
8. Heat a metal ladle and add the remaining Kirsch or brandy. Carefully set light to it and pour over the pineapple.
9. Serve the pineapple as soon as the flames die down, with pouring or whipping cream.

LEFT: Pineapple with caramel sauce. RIGHT: Mocha fondue

MOCHA FONDUE

Serves 6
600 ml (1 pint) single cream
3 tablespoons freshly ground coffee or 2 tablespoons instant coffee
5 egg yolks
50 g (2 oz) caster sugar
To dip:
chunks of peeled banana
marshmallows

Preparation time: about 5 minutes, plus standing
Cooking time: about 15 minutes

Two tablespoons instant coffee can be used to flavour this fondue, but ground coffee gives a much better result. This fondue contains eggs and it is important that it does not become too hot, otherwise it will curdle. The best way of avoiding this is to use a cheese fondue pan, one third filled with simmering water, and to have the actual fondue in an ovenproof bowl that will fit neatly over the top – make sure that the bowl fits really well.

1. Heat the cream in a saucepan until it is quite hot, but do not boil.
2. Pour the cream on to the ground coffee. Cover and leave to steep in a cool place for 3-4 hours. Strain the cream.
3. Heat the coffee-flavoured cream in the top of a double saucepan.
4. Beat the egg yolks with the sugar. Pour on the hot cream and beat in.
5. Return to the top of the double saucepan and cook, stirring, until the fondue mixture will coat the back of a wooden spoon.
6. Ⓣ Transfer the fondue to an ovenproof bowl and place over the fondue pan of simmering water.
7. Serve with banana and marshmallows to dip.

Serving Mocha fondue
If you are making this for young children, the safest way of serving it is to ladle it into small warmed soup bowls, so that each person has their own portion. Serve separate plates with the dunks on, e.g. chunks of banana, marshmallows, etc. Children usually have a sweeter tooth than adults, and it may be advisable to provide brown sugar or honey for stirring into each portion; watch the children carefully to make sure that they do not overdo it.

FOOD ON A SKEWER

MIDDLE EASTERN-STYLE KEBABS

1 medium aubergine
salt
8 button onions, peeled
2 medium courgettes, cut into rings 1 cm (½ inch) thick
1 red pepper, cored, seeded and cut into cubes
8 button or small tomatoes
150 ml (¼ pint) plain unsweetened yogurt
1 garlic clove, peeled and crushed
½ teaspoon ground ginger
3 tablespoons olive oil
salt
freshly ground black pepper
To serve:
slices of Mozzarella or Feta cheese
olive oil

Preparation time: 20 minutes, plus chilling and standing
Cooking time: about 13 minutes

These kebabs are rather crunchy – if you prefer vegetables that are more tender, then blanch them first.

1. Cut the aubergine roughly into 2.5 cm (1 inch) cubes. Put into a colander and sprinkle generously with salt. Leave to stand for 30 minutes.
2. Simmer the button onions in boiling water for 5 minutes. Drain the onions.
3. Rinse the aubergine cubes and pat dry on paper towels.
4. Thread the aubergine, onions, courgettes, red pepper and tomatoes on to four medium kebab skewers.
5. Mix the yogurt with the garlic, ginger, oil, and salt and pepper to taste.
6. Place the kebabs in a large shallow dish. Spoon over the yogurt baste and chill for 3 hours.
7. Remove the kebabs from the baste, shaking gently to allow the excess baste to drip off.
8. Place the kebabs on the rack of the grill pan. Place under a preheated grill and cook the kebabs for about 4 minutes on each side, brushing with a little extra baste during cooking.
9. Serve hot, with a salad of slices of Mozzarella or Feta cheese, sprinkled with olive oil.

MIXED FRUIT KEBABS

150 ml (¼ pint) fresh orange juice
juice of 2 lemons
50 g (2 oz) caster sugar
1 pear, peeled, cored and cut into 8 sections
2 small firm bananas, peeled and each cut into 4 chunks
2 slices of fresh or canned pineapple, cut into sizeable chunks
8 stoned cherries or seeded grapes
4 small pieces of preserved stem ginger
2 tablespoons melted honey
demerara sugar, for sprinkling
2 tablespoons flaked almonds
Coconut cream:
3 tablespoons desiccated coconut
4 tablespoons boiling water
150 ml (¼ pint) double cream, whipped

Preparation time: 20-25 minutes, plus standing
Cooking time: 3-4 minutes

This could be called 'fruit salad on a stick'! Children will love it as a fun pudding, and it is equally suitable for serving at a dinner party.

1. To make the Coconut cream, mix the desiccated coconut with the boiling water. Leave to stand for 30 minutes. Strain through a sieve, pressing on the coconut to extract the flavour. Whisk the 'coconut milk' into the thickly whipped cream. This can be prepared in advance.
2. Mix the orange juice with the lemon juice and caster sugar.
3. Add the pear, bananas, pineapple, cherries and ginger, and stir until evenly coated in the fruit juice mixture—this will prevent unnecessary discoloration of the fruit.
4. Drain the fruits thoroughly and thread alternately on to 4 kebab skewers.
5. Put the fruit kebabs on the rack of the grill pan. Brush with melted honey and sprinkle with demerara sugar and almonds.
6. Place under a preheated grill and cook for 3-4 minutes until lightly golden.
7. Serve immediately with the Coconut cream.

FROM THE FRONT: Mixed fruit kebabs; Middle Eastern-style kebabs

SKEWERED SAUSAGE MEATBALLS

4 tablespoons sage and onion stuffing mix
8 tablespoons boiling water
450 g (1 lb) pork sausage meat
1 egg yolk
salt
freshly ground black pepper
2 red-skinned apples, halved, cored and cut into wedges
juice of 1 lemon
oil, for brushing

Preparation time: 20 minutes, plus chilling
Cooking time: 10-12 minutes

1. Mix the dry stuffing mix with the boiling water and leave to stand until the water has been absorbed.
2. Mix the stuffing with the sausage meat, egg yolk, and salt and pepper to taste.
3. Form into small balls, about the size of a chestnut, then chill for 1 hour.
4. Toss the wedges of apple in lemon juice.
5. Thread the sausage meatballs and apple wedges alternately on to 4 kebab skewers.
6. Put on the rack of the grill pan. Brush with oil. Place under a preheated grill for 5 minutes. Turn, brush with oil and cook for a further 5-6 minutes.

FROM THE FRONT: Skewered sausage meatballs; Chicken liver and water chestnut kebabs

BRUNCH KEBABS

350 g (12 oz) black pudding
12 rashers streaky bacon
16 button mushrooms or small flat mushrooms
oil, to brush
salt
freshly ground black pepper
2 medium cooking apples, peeled, cored and cut into 5 mm
   (¼ inch) thick rings
50 g (2 oz) butter, melted

Preparation time: 15 minutes
Cooking time: 6 minutes

1. Cut the black pudding into 12 even-sized slices. Wrap each one in a rasher of bacon.
2. Thread 3 black pudding and bacon rolls on to each of 4 kebab skewers, alternately with 4 button mushrooms.
3. Brush the kebabs generously with oil and sprinkle with salt and pepper.
4. Put the kebabs on the rack of the grill pan. Place under a preheated grill and cook for about 3 minutes. Turn the kebabs and cook for a further 3 minutes.
5. Meanwhile prepare the buttered apple rings: put the apple rings into a large shallow pan with the melted butter. Cook gently for 1 minute. Flip the apple rings over and cook briskly for a further 1-2 minutes.
6. Serve the kebabs on a bed of buttered apple rings.

CHICKEN LIVER AND WATER CHESTNUT KEBABS

450 g (1 lb) chicken livers, rinsed and dried
8 thin rashers unsmoked streaky bacon
8 canned water chestnuts, halved if large
2 tablespoons soy sauce
4 tablespoons oil
salt
freshly ground black pepper

Preparation time: 15 minutes
Cooking time: 8-10 minutes

1. Cut the chicken livers into 16 even-sized pieces.
2. Cut the bacon rashers in half crossways.
3. Roll up each piece of chicken liver and half water chestnut in a half rasher of bacon.
4. Thread on to 4 kebab skewers.
5. Mix soy sauce with the oil, salt and pepper.
6. Put the kebabs on the rack of the grill pan. Spoon the soy sauce mixture over the prepared kebabs.
7. Place under a preheated moderately hot grill and cook for 4-5 minutes. Turn the kebabs, spoon over remaining sauce and cook for a further 4-5 minutes.

Chicken livers

When patting chicken livers dry use a clean cloth rather than paper towels, which are likely to stick to the livers. The pieces of bacon will roll more easily if you stretch them slightly, by running the blade of a round-bladed knife the length of the bacon. Calves' liver can be substituted for chicken livers, if preferred, but it does make the dish more expensive. As well as serving plain boiled rice or risotto as an accompaniment, try a salad based on bean sprouts.

SWEETBREADS EN BROCHETTE

500 g (1¼ lb) lamb's sweetbreads
salt
freshly ground black pepper
6 tablespoons fine fresh white breadcrumbs
finely grated rind of ½ lemon
1 tablespoon flour
melted butter
Lemon cream sauce:
150 ml (¼ pint) double cream
grated rind of ½ lemon
2 tablespoons finely chopped fresh parsley

Preparation time: 20-25 minutes
Cooking time: 10 minutes

1. Soak the sweetbreads in warm water for 10 minutes.
2. Drain the sweetbreads and put into a pan with sufficient cold water to cover. Bring to the boil and simmer for 1 minute. Remove any loose membrane.
3. Drain the sweetbreads and cut into even-sized pieces, roughly 2 cm (¾ inch) square.
4. Mix together the salt, pepper, breadcrumbs and lemon rind.
5. Toss the prepared sweetbreads lightly in flour and then in melted butter. Then roll them in the crumb mixture to give an even coating.
6. Thread on to 4 kebab skewers. Put on the rack of the grill pan. Brush with extra melted butter.
7. Place under a preheated grill and cook for about 4 minutes. Turn the kebabs and brush with a little extra melted butter. Cook for a further 4 minutes until tender.
8. For the Lemon cream sauce, heat the cream without boiling and stir in the lemon rind, parsley and salt and pepper to taste. Serve the sweetbreads with the sauce, handed separately.

MIXED GRILL ON A SKEWER

225 g (8 oz) lamb fillet, cut into 2.5 cm (1 inch) cubes
4 lamb's kidneys, skinned, halved, cored and quartered
12 small cocktail sausages
12 even-sized button mushrooms
Baste:
1 tablespoon Worcestershire sauce
3 tablespoons tomato chutney
2 tablespoons oil
1 garlic clove, peeled and crushed
juice of ½ lemon
salt
freshly ground black pepper

Preparation time: about 10 minutes
Cooking time: about 10 minutes

1. Thread the cubed lamb, kidneys, cocktail sausages and button mushrooms alternately on to 4 long kebab skewers.
2. For the baste, mix together the remaining ingredients.
3. Put the kebabs on the rack of the grill pan. Brush or spread half the well flavoured baste over the kebabs.
4. Place under a preheated moderately hot grill and cook for 5 minutes.
5. Turn the kebabs over and brush with more baste. Cook for a further 5 minutes until the meats are tender.
6. Serve with sauté potatoes and a green vegetable.

PLAICE AND ANCHOVY ROLL-UPS

12 small plaice fillets
anchovy paste, for spreading
flour, for dusting
Coating batter:
100 g (4 oz) plain flour
salt
freshly ground black pepper
1 egg
150 ml (¼ pint) milk
oil, for deep frying
Parsley mayonnaise:
150 ml (¼ pint) mayonnaise
3 tablespoons soured cream
3 tablespoons finely chopped fresh parsley

Preparation time: 25-30 minutes
Cooking time: 5-6 minutes

1. Cut each plaice fillet in half crossways.
2. Spread thinly on one side with anchovy paste and roll up Swiss roll fashion.
3. Thread 6 plaice rolls on to each of 4 kebab skewers.
4. Dust lightly on all sides with flour.
5. For the batter, sift the flour with salt and pepper to taste into a bowl. Make a well in the centre, add the egg and a little of the milk. Beat until smooth, adding the rest of the milk.
6. Pass each skewer through the batter to give a thin, even coating – the easiest way to do this is to hold each kebab over a shallow dish and to spoon the batter over.
7. Fill a large pan one third full of oil and heat to 190°C (375°F), or until a cube of bread browns in 30 seconds. Lower the skewers into the hot oil and fry steadily for 5-6 minutes until crisp and golden. Drain on paper towels.
8. For the Parsley mayonnaise, mix together the remaining ingredients. Serve with the roll-ups.

SIMPLE FISH KEBABS

450 g (1 lb) firm textured white fish (e.g. cod, halibut, monkfish, etc)
4 tablespoons lime or lemon juice
6 tablespoons olive oil
salt
freshly ground black pepper
1 tablespoon chopped fresh rosemary or 1 teaspoon dried
4 small onions, peeled and cut into thick rings
1 lemon, cut into thin wedges

Preparation time: 15 minutes, plus chilling
Cooking time: 6-8 minutes

You need a firm textured fish to use for kebabs, so that it does not fall to pieces during cooking. Fish kebabs keep their shape better if they are cooked on a baking sheet or large shallow flameproof dish, rather than the rack of a grill pan.

1. Cut the fish into 2.5 cm (1 inch) cubes. Put the fish cubes into a shallow dish.
2. Mix the lime juice with the oil, salt and pepper to taste, and the rosemary. Spoon over the fish. Cover and chill for 4 hours.
3. Thread the fish cubes on to 4 kebab skewers alternately with the onion rings and lemon wedges. Put on a baking sheet or shallow flameproof dish. Brush with the marinade.
4. Place under a preheated grill and cook for 3-4 minutes on one side. Turn the kebabs, brush again with the marinade and cook for a further 3-4 minutes.
5. Serve with warm pitta bread and a green salad.

CLOCKWISE FROM THE FRONT: Plaice and anchovy roll-ups; Mixed grill on a skewer; Simple fish kebabs

SPATCHCOCK CHICKEN

Serves 2

2 poussins, cleaned
6 tablespoons oil
1 tablespoon Worcestershire sauce
2 garlic cloves, peeled and crushed
juice of ½ lemon
1 tablespoon French mustard
salt
freshly ground black pepper

Preparation time: about 30 minutes, plus chilling
Cooking time: about 20 minutes

Once the poussins have been split and flattened they are quite large, and this is the reason it is suggested that you only cook this dish for 2 people – you would need a very large grill pan to take 4 prepared poussins. You could, however, prepare the poussins for more people if you were cooking them on a barbecue.

1. Place the poussins on a board, breasts downwards.
2. Cut through the backbone, from one end of the poussin to the other, with poultry shears or a sharp knife.
3. Remove the backbone completely.
4. Open out each poussin and place skin side uppermost on a chopping board. Beat with a meat mallet or rolling pin to flatten each poussin – not so hard that it completely splinters the bones and tears the flesh.
5. Fold the wing tips under the wings, so that they lie flat. Cut off the feet.
6. Insert 2 skewers, criss-cross fashion, through the poussins to hold them rigid.
7. Place the prepared poussins in a shallow dish.
8. Mix together the oil, Worcestershire sauce, garlic, lemon juice, mustard, and salt and pepper to taste. Spoon over the poussins. Cover and chill for 4-6 hours, or preferably overnight.
9. Put the poussins, skin side down, on the rack of the grill pan. Place under a preheated fairly hot grill and cook for 10 minutes.
10. Turn the poussins and baste with any spare marinade. Cook for a further 10 minutes until tender.

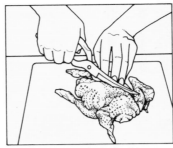

1. Cutting through the backbone with poultry shears.

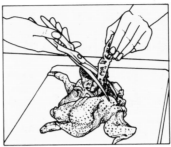

2. Removing the backbone.

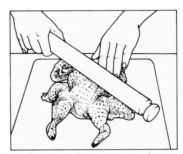

3. Flattening the poussin with a rolling pin or mallet.

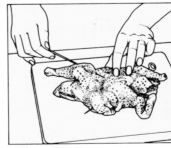

4. Skewering the poussin crosswise.

SPECIAL BEEF KEBABS

450 g (1 lb) lean beef (rump, entrecôte steak, etc)
2 medium courgettes, about 225 g (8 oz), sliced
1 small orange, cut into 8 wedges
Marinade:
6 tablespoons oil
grated rind of 1 orange
2 tablespoons brandy
2 tablespoons chopped fresh rosemary or 2 teaspoons dried
1 garlic clove, peeled and crushed
salt
freshly ground black pepper

Preparation time: 15 minutes, plus chilling
Cooking time: 10-12 minutes

1. Cut the beef into 2.5 cm (1 inch) cubes.
2. For the marinade, mix the ingredients together.
3. Put the cubed beef into a shallow dish and spoon the marinade over. Cover and chill for 4 hours.
4. Remove the beef from the marinade and drain.
5. Thread the beef cubes on to 4 kebab skewers alternately with the slices of courgette and wedges of orange.
6. Put the kebabs on the rack of the grill pan. Brush with the marinade. Place under a preheated grill and cook for 5-6 minutes.
7. Turn the kebabs and brush with more marinade. Cook for a further 5-6 minutes.
8. Serve hot with rice and a salad.

VEAL AND PRUNE KEBABS

12 large pitted prunes
about 150 ml (¼ pint) dry white wine
500 g (1¼ lb) lean veal, in one piece
3 slices ham
3 tablespoons clear honey
3 tablespoons white wine vinegar
salt
freshly ground black pepper
oil

Preparation time: about 20 minutes, plus standing overnight
Cooking time: 14 minutes

PORK SATAY

Serves 6
3 tablespoons smooth or crunchy peanut butter
2 tablespoons soy sauce
1 tablespoon vinegar
1 tablespoon stock or water
salt
freshly ground black pepper
1 teaspoon curry powder
450 g (1 lb) pork fillet
2 lemons, cut into wedges, to serve

Preparation time: 10-15 minutes, plus chilling
Cooking time: about 6 minutes

Satay are usually served as an appetizer with drinks, or as part of an hors d'oeuvre, so you need to use small metal skewers – not the long kebab skewers.

1. Put the peanut butter, soy sauce, vinegar, stock or water, a little salt and some pepper to taste, and the curry powder into a pan. Stir over a gentle heat until creamy. Allow to cool.
2. Cut the pork fillet into 1 cm (½ inch) cubes.
3. Stir the pork fillet cubes into the peanut baste. Cover and chill for 4 hours.
4. Thread on to 12 small metal skewers. Put on the rack of the grill pan.
5. Place under a preheated grill and cook for about 2 minutes. Turn the satay skewers and cook for a further 2 minutes.
6. Serve with the lemon wedges.

1. Place the prunes in a shallow dish and add sufficient white wine to cover. Leave to stand overnight, or until well plumped.
2. Cut the veal into 2.5 cm (1 inch) cubes.
3. Cut each slice of ham into 4 strips. Roll up each plumped prune in a strip of ham.
4. Thread the cubed veal and prune and ham rolls on to 4 kebab skewers.
5. Heat the honey and wine vinegar in a small pan until the honey has dissolved. Season to taste.
6. Brush the threaded kebabs first with oil and then with the honey baste.
7. Place the kebabs on the rack of the grill pan. Place under a preheated grill and cook for about 6 minutes on each side, brushing the kebabs with the honey baste halfway through cooking.

FROM THE FRONT: Special beef kebabs; Pork satay

HAM AND CHEESE KEBABS

1 thick slice cooked ham, about 350 g (12 oz) in weight and
   2.5 cm (1 inch) thick
225 g (8 oz) Edam cheese
flour, for dusting
1 egg, beaten
3 tablespoons fine fresh white breadcrumbs
salt
freshly ground black pepper
4 tablespoons redcurrant jelly
juice of ½ orange

Preparation time: 25 minutes
Cooking time: 8-9 minutes

1. Cut the ham into 2.5 cm (1 inch) cubes.
2. Cut the cheese into 2 cm (¾ inch) cubes.
3. Dust the cheese cubes lightly with flour. Dip into beaten egg and then roll in the breadcrumbs to give an even coating.
4. Thread the ham and crumbed cheese cubes alternately on to 4 kebab skewers. Place on the rack of the grill pan and add salt and pepper.
5. Melt the redcurrant jelly with the orange juice in a pan. Spoon a little of the redcurrant glaze over each prepared kebab.
6. Place under a preheated grill and cook for about 4 minutes. Turn the kebabs and spoon over a little more of the redcurrant glaze. Cook for a further 4 minutes.
7. Serve hot with Orange and watercress salad (see page 12).

LEFT: Ham and cheese kebabs. RIGHT: Skewered meatballs

SKEWERED MEATBALLS

450 g (1 lb) lamb fillet, minced
1 medium onion, peeled and finely chopped or grated
2 teaspoons fresh thyme or ¼ teaspoon dried
salt
freshly ground black pepper
2 garlic cloves, peeled and crushed
2 egg yolks
1 large red pepper, halved, cored and seeded
1 large green pepper, halved, cored and seeded
5 tablespoons oil
generous pinch of ground ginger
pinch of ground turmeric
Yogurt and cucumber sauce:
½ cucumber, peeled and grated
½ teaspoon dill seed
generous pinch of caster sugar
150 ml (¼ pint) plain unsweetened yogurt
1 tablespoon chopped fresh mint

**Preparation time: about 25 minutes, plus chilling
Cooking time: 12-14 minutes**

1. Mix the minced lamb with the onion, thyme, salt and pepper, garlic and egg yolks.
2. Form into 24 small meatballs about the size of a chestnut. Cover and chill for 3-4 hours, to firm up the texture of the meatballs.
3. Cut the peppers into pieces roughly 2.5 cm (1 inch) square.
4. Thread the prepared meatballs and pieces of pepper alternately on to 4 kebab skewers. Put into a shallow dish.
5. Mix the oil with the ginger, turmeric, and salt and pepper to taste. Brush the prepared kebabs with the flavoured oil. Cover and chill for a further hour.
6. For the yogurt and cucumber sauce, squeeze the grated cucumber in a piece of muslin to remove excess moisture. Mix the cucumber with the dill, sugar, yogurt, mint, and salt and pepper to taste.
7. Put the kebabs on the rack of the grill pan and brush with the flavoured oil. Place under a preheated grill and cook for 6-8 minutes.
8. Turn the kebabs, brushing again with the flavoured oil, and cook for a further 6 minutes. Serve hot with the Yogurt and cucumber sauce and a salad.

SPECIAL SANDWICHES

PITTA AND SALAMI SPECIALS

4 pieces large pitta bread
heart of 1 Cos lettuce, shredded
1 medium onion, peeled and not too finely chopped
olive oil, for sprinkling
175 g (6 oz) Feta or Mozzarella cheese, cubed
100 g (4 oz) salami, thinly sliced
50 g (2 oz) stoned black olives, chopped
salt
freshly ground black pepper

Preparation time: 3 minutes
Cooking time: 5 minutes
Oven: 180°C, 350°F, Gas Mark 4

1. Wrap the pieces of pitta bread loosely in an envelope of foil. Place in a preheated oven and heat through for 5 minutes.
2. Make a split lengthways down one side of each piece of pitta bread, to form a pocket.
3. Fill with a layer of shredded lettuce and a little chopped onion. Dribble a little olive oil over the lettuce and onion.
4. Add some cubed cheese, salami and chopped olives to each pitta bread sandwich, with salt and pepper to taste. The pitta bread must be filled quickly, otherwise it will cool.
5. Serve while the bread is still warm.

SMOKED SALMON RAREBIT

Serves 4
225 g (8 oz) cheese, grated
2 eggs, separated
1 teaspoon French mustard
salt
freshly ground black pepper
3 tablespoons milk
75 g (3 oz) smoked salmon trimmings, finely chopped
4 large slices wholemeal bread

Preparation time: 10 minutes
Cooking time: 4-5 minutes

1. Mix the grated cheese with the egg yolks, French mustard, salt and pepper to taste, milk and the chopped smoked salmon.
2. Whisk the egg whites until stiff and fold lightly but thoroughly into the cheese mixture.
3. Toast the bread on one side only.
4. Divide the cheese mixture between the 4 slices of bread, spreading it evenly on the untoasted sides of the bread.
5. Place under a preheated moderately hot grill and cook until the cheese topping has risen and is golden brown. Serve hot.

PUMPERNICKEL PARTY SNACKS

Makes 12
36 cocktail rounds of pumpernickel
275 g (10 oz) full fat soft cheese
1 tablespoon brandy
salt
freshly ground black pepper
2 tablespoons finely chopped walnuts or hazelnuts
halved black grapes or walnut halves, to garnish

Preparation time: 15 minutes

1. Match up the rounds of pumpernickel as they do tend to vary in shape – you need 3 for each party snack sandwich.
2. Mix the cheese with the brandy, salt and pepper to taste, and the chopped nuts.
3. Spread two thirds of the pumpernickel rounds evenly with the cheese mixture, reserving a little for securing the garnish.
4. Assemble each party snack sandwich, using two rounds of cheese topped pumpernickel and one round plain – placing the plain round in the centre.
5. Fix a halved grape or walnut on top of each one, securing it with a little cheese mixture.

FROM THE FRONT: Pitta and salami specials; Smoked salmon rarebit; Pumpernickel party snacks

SMORGASBORD PINWHEEL

Serves 8

1 slice bread, 23-25 cm (9-10 inches) in diameter, and 2 cm
(¾ inch) thick
softened butter, for spreading
450 g (1 lb) full fat soft cheese
100 g (4 oz) Danish blue cheese, finely crumbled
salt
freshly ground black pepper
3 tablespoons mayonnaise
1 × 75 g (3 oz) jar red lumpfish roe
1 × 75 g (3 oz) jar black lumpfish roe
225 g (8 oz) stuffed olives, sliced
paprika, for sprinkling (optional)

Preparation time: 25 minutes

You need a very large slice of bread for this party-style
open sandwich – choose a large cottage loaf, or similar
shaped round loaf, preferably 23-25 cm (9-10 inches)
in diameter. Cut a slice 2 cm (¾ inch) thick from the
thickest part of the loaf.

1. Spread the bread slice with a thin even layer of
butter and put it on to a flat board or platter.
2. Beat half the soft cheese in a bowl until creamy. Mix
with the crumbled blue cheese and salt and pepper to
taste.
3. Spread the cheese mixture evenly over the bread
circle.
4. Mix the remaining cream cheese with the mayonnaise.
5. Mark the top of the bread circle into 8 equal sections, with the blade of a sharp knife.
6. Using a piping bag fitted with a star nozzle, pipe the
cream cheese and mayonnaise mixture into rosettes
along the marked lines and around the outer edge of
the circle of bread.
7. Fill 4 alternate sections with sliced olives, 2 sections with red lumpfish roe and 2 with black roe.
8. Sprinkle the cheese with paprika, if liked.

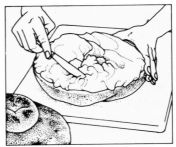

1. Spreading the cheese mixture
over the bread.

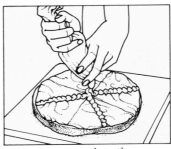

2. Marking off the sections with
the blade of a knife.

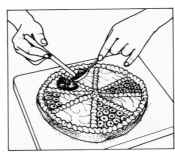

3. Piping rosettes along the
marked lines.

4. Filling the sections with roe and
sliced olives.

FISHERMEN'S STICKS

Serves 6
12 fish fingers
melted butter or oil
salt
freshly ground black pepper
6 long crusty bread rolls
tomato ketchup
2 small packets potato crisps
3 tomatoes, cut into thin wedges

Preparation time: 5 minutes
Cooking time: 15 minutes
Oven: 190°C, 375°F, Gas Mark 5

This makes an excellent party snack for older children – the rolls look appetizing, and I have yet to meet a child who does not like fish fingers!

1. Brush the fish fingers with melted butter or oil. Place under a preheated moderately hot grill and cook for 8-10 minutes, turning them once. Add salt and pepper to taste.
2. Split the rolls lengthways, without cutting them right through. Brush inside each roll with melted butter or oil and put on a baking sheet. Place in a preheated oven and bake for 5 minutes.
3. Spread the cut surface of the rolls with ketchup. Fill each one with a layer of potato crisps, 2 cooked fish fingers and a few tomato wedges. Serve immediately.

BAKED SARDINE TOASTS

2 eggs
1 tablespoon Worcestershire sauce
salt
freshly ground black pepper
4 slices bread, 1 cm (½ inch) thick
2 × 200 g (7 oz) can sardines in oil
grated rind of ½ lemon
225 g (8 oz) herb flavoured full fat soft cheese
2 tablespoons mayonnaise
1 small onion, peeled and finely chopped

Preparation time: 15 minutes
Cooking time: 20 minutes
Oven: 190°C, 375°F, Gas Mark 5

1. Beat the eggs in a bowl with the Worcestershire sauce and salt and pepper to taste.
2. Dip both sides of the bread slices into the egg mixture, and put on a lightly greased baking sheet. Place in a preheated oven and bake for 5 minutes.
3. Mash the sardines with the lemon rind and salt and pepper to taste. Spread evenly over each slice of baked bread.
4. Beat the cheese with a wooden spoon to soften and then beat in the mayonnaise and onion. Spread the cheese mixture evenly over the sardines.
5. Return to the oven and bake the toasts for about 15 minutes until the topping turns golden. Serve immediately.

AVOCADO AND PRAWN ROLLS

4 wholemeal rolls
softened butter, for spreading
1 ripe avocado pear, halved, stoned and peeled
juice of 1 lemon
salt
freshly ground black pepper
175 g (6 oz) peeled prawns
4 tablespoons mayonnaise
cayenne pepper
lettuce leaves
To garnish:
4 unpeeled prawns
4 parsley sprigs

Preparation time: 15-20 minutes

1. Cut each roll into 3 layers of even depth.
2. Spread one cut surface of each layer with butter.
3. Cut the avocado flesh into thin slices and toss in lemon juice with salt and pepper to taste.
4. Mix the peeled prawns with the mayonnaise, a little cayenne pepper and salt and black pepper to taste.
5. Reassemble the split rolls into their original shape, adding avocado slices, prawns and a little lettuce to each layer.
6. Garnish each filled roll with an unpeeled prawn and parsley sprig.

LEFT: Baked sardine toasts. RIGHT: Smoked haddock triangles

SMOKED HADDOCK TRIANGLES

Makes 16

450 g (1 lb) smoked haddock fillet
milk, to cover
1 bay leaf
salt
freshly ground black pepper
mayonnaise, for binding and spreading
grated rind of 1 lemon
8 large slices white bread
4 large slices brown bread
softened butter, for spreading
chopped fresh parsley
small lemon fans, to garnish

Preparation time: 25 minutes
Cooking time: 8 minutes

1. Put the smoked haddock into a shallow pan with sufficient milk to half cover, the bay leaf and salt and pepper to taste. Poach gently until the fish is just tender.

2. Drain the fish. Discard any skin and bone and flake the flesh. Allow to cool.

3. Mix the flaked fish with sufficient mayonnaise to bind. Add salt and pepper to taste and mix with the lemon rind.

4. Spread the white and brown bread evenly with butter.

5. Using 2 slices of white bread and 1 slice of brown bread for each round of sandwiches, sandwich together with the fish mixture – placing the brown slice in the centre of the sandwich.

6. Cut off the crusts and cut each round of sandwiches into 4 triangles.

7. Spread the tops of each triangular sandwich lightly with mayonnaise and dip into chopped parsley.

8. Garnish the triangles with small lemon fans.

BEEF AND COLESLAW CLUB SANDWICH

Makes 1
3 slices hot toast
softened butter, for spreading
10-12 thin slices cucumber
2 tablespoons coleslaw
creamed horseradish, for spreading
2 slices lean rare roast beef
To garnish:
tomato wedges
sprigs of watercress

Preparation time: 3 minutes
Cooking time: 2 minutes

You need to work quickly when assembling this sandwich, so that the toast does not get too cold.

1. Spread the toast on one side only with butter.
2. Top one slice of toast with a layer of cucumber and coleslaw. Cover with a second slice of toast spread with horseradish.
3. Arrange the sliced beef on top of the horseradish, and place the third slice of toast on top, buttered side down.
4. Cut the sandwich in half diagonally and garnish with tomato and watercress.

PÂTÉ BEEHIVES

Makes 8
14 large slices wholemeal bread from a sliced loaf
350 g (12 oz) smooth pâté
melted butter, for brushing
4 tablespoons chopped fresh parsley
4 tablespoons chopped toasted nuts
2 stuffed olives, sliced

Preparation time: 30 minutes, plus chilling

These attractive sandwiches are made up using 3 layers of bread for each one, cut in different diameter circles. You should be able to get one 6 cm (2½ inch) circle from 1 slice of bread; two 5 cm (2 inch) circles from 1 slice; and four 4 cm (1½ inch) circles from 1 slice.

1. Cut 8 circles of bread 6 cm (2½ inches) in diameter, 8 circles 5 cm (2 inches) in diameter, and 8 circles 4 cm (1½ inches) in diameter.
2. Spread the large circles with two thirds of the pâté, and the medium-size circles, i.e. 5 cm (2 inch), with the remaining pâté.

BLUE CHEESE SPECIAL

Makes 1
2 rashers bacon
2 large slices brown bread, from a sliced loaf
softened butter, for spreading
50 g (2 oz) Danish blue cheese, crumbled
1 tablespoon mayonnaise
salt
freshly ground black pepper

Preparation time: 5 minutes
Cooking time: 8-9 minutes

1. Place the bacon under a preheated moderately hot grill and cook until it is crisp. Chop the bacon.
2. Spread both slices of bread thinly but evenly with butter.
3. Place one slice of bread, buttered side down, on the rack of the grill.
4. Mix the chopped bacon with the crumbled cheese, mayonnaise and salt and pepper to taste.
5. Spread the cheese mixture evenly over the slice of bread on the rack. Top with the other slice, buttered side uppermost. Press the slices of bread gently together.
6. Place the sandwich under a preheated moderately hot grill and cook for 4-5 minutes, turning the sandwich once. Serve immediately.

3. To assemble the beehives, sit a medium size circle of bread on top of each large circle, and one of the small circles right at the top.
4. Smooth around the edges, using a round bladed knife, to even off the pâté. Chill for 30 minutes.
5. Brush the beehives with melted butter. Coat 4 of the beehives with chopped parsley, and 4 with toasted nuts.
6. Fix an olive slice on top of each one.

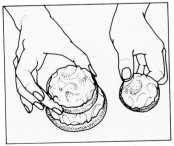 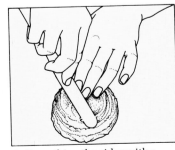

1. Assembling the pâté beehive.

2. Smoothing the sides with a round-bladed knife.

LEFT: Beef and coleslaw club sandwich. RIGHT: Pâté beehives

CHICKEN AND ALMOND ROUNDELS

Makes 8
8 large slices white bread, from a sliced loaf
8 large slices brown bread, from a sliced loaf
softened butter, for spreading
175 g (6 oz) cooked boned chicken, finely chopped
2 tablespoons soured cream
25 g (1 oz) blanched almonds, toasted and chopped
salt
freshly ground black pepper
redcurrant jelly, for topping

Preparation time: 20-25 minutes

1. Cut a round from each slice of bread, using a large fluted pastry cutter, 9 cm (3½ inches) in diameter.
2. Using a 5 cm (2 inch) diameter pastry cutter, cut out the centre from each white circle of bread, leaving a ring shape.
3. Spread the circles of brown bread with butter.
4. Mix the chopped chicken with the soured cream, almonds and salt and pepper to taste.
5. Spread the brown circles of bread with the chicken mixture and sandwich together with the rings of white bread.
6. Spoon a little redcurrant jelly into the 'hole' in the top of each sandwich.

TOASTED HAM AND CHEESE SANDWICH

Makes 1
2 large slices white bread, from a sliced loaf
softened butter, for spreading
French mustard, for spreading
50 g (2 oz) cheese, grated
1 slice of ham
salt
freshly ground black pepper

Preparation time: 5 minutes
Cooking time: 4-5 minutes

1. Spread both slices of bread thinly but evenly with butter and then spread them with a thin layer of French mustard.
2. Place one slice of bread, buttered side down, on the rack of the grill.
3. Put half the grated cheese on to the slice of bread on the rack. Top with the slice of ham, the remaining grated cheese and salt and pepper to taste.
4. Top with the other slice of bread, buttered side uppermost. Press the slices of bread gently together.
5. Place the sandwich under a preheated moderately hot grill and cook for 4-5 minutes, turning the sandwich once. Serve immediately.

TOASTED TUNA AND EGG SANDWICH

Makes 1
2 large slices white bread, from a sliced loaf
softened butter, for spreading
1 hard-boiled egg, chopped
1 spring onion, trimmed and chopped
salt
freshly ground black pepper
1 tablespoon flaked tuna
2 tablespoons mayonnaise

Preparation time: 5 minutes
Cooking time: 4-5 minutes

1. Spread both slices of bread thinly but evenly with butter.
2. Place one slice of bread, buttered side down, on the rack of the grill.
3. Mix the hard-boiled egg with the spring onion, salt and pepper to taste, tuna and mayonnaise.
4. Spread the tuna and egg mixture evenly over the slice of bread on the rack. Top with the other slice, buttered side uppermost. Press the slices of bread gently together.
5. Place the sandwich under a preheated moderately hot grill and cook for 4-5 minutes, turning the sandwich once. Serve immediately.

TOASTED CHICKEN, SWEETCORN AND CELERY SANDWICH

Makes 1
2 large slices brown bread, from a sliced loaf
softened butter, for spreading
50 g (2 oz) cooked chicken, chopped
2 tablespoons sweetcorn relish
1 tablespoon finely chopped celery
salt
freshly ground black pepper

Preparation time: 5 minutes
Cooking time: 5 minutes

1. Spread both slices of bread thinly but evenly with butter.
2. Place one slice of bread, buttered side down, on the rack of the grill.
3. Mix the chicken with the sweetcorn relish, celery and salt and pepper to taste.
4. Spread the chicken mixture evenly over the slice of bread on the rack. Top with the other slice, buttered side uppermost. Press the slices of bread gently together.
5. Place the sandwich under a preheated moderately hot grill and cook for 4-5 minutes, turning the sandwich once. Serve immediately.

BURGER BRUNCH

4 thin beefburgers, either bought or homemade
oil, for brushing
2 baps
4 tablespoons tomato chutney
salt
freshly ground black pepper
225 g (8 oz) mashed potato
100 g (4 oz) Cheddar cheese, grated

Preparation time: 5 minutes
Cooking time: about 30 minutes
Oven: 190°C, 375°F, Gas Mark 5

1. Brush the burgers with oil. Place under a preheated grill and cook for about 3 minutes on each side.
2. Split the baps in half and toast the cut surfaces lightly.
3. Spread the baps with tomato chutney and top each with a cooked burger. Add salt and pepper to taste.
4. Fork some mashed potato over the top of each burger and sprinkle with grated cheese.
5. Place in a preheated oven and bake for about 15 minutes until the potato and cheese topping is golden. Serve hot.

HOT DOG TOASTIES

Makes 1
1 tablespoon oil
1 small onion, peeled and cut into thin rings
2 large slices white bread, from a sliced loaf
softened butter, for spreading
1 frankfurter, cut into rounds
1 tablespoon mustard pickle
salt
freshly ground black pepper

Preparation time: 5 minutes
Cooking time: 9-10 minutes

1. Heat the oil in a pan, add the onion rings and fry gently until tender and lightly golden.
2. Spread both slices of bread thinly but evenly with butter.
3. Place one slice of bread, buttered side down, on the rack of the grill.
4. Mix the onion rings with the frankfurter, pickle and salt and pepper to taste.
5. Spread the frankfurter and onion mixture evenly over the slice of bread on the rack. Top with the other slice, buttered side uppermost. Press the slices of bread gently together.
6. Place the sandwich under a preheated moderately hot grill and cook for 4-5 minutes, turning the sandwich once. Serve immediately.

STEAK AND FRIED EGG TOAST

Makes 1
25 g (1 oz) butter
1 thin rump or entrecôte steak, about 100 g (4 oz)
salt
freshly ground black pepper
oil, for frying
2 thin slices white bread
1 egg
French mustard, for spreading
watercress, to garnish

Preparation time: 3-4 minutes
Cooking time: 6-8 minutes

A perfect sandwich to choose when you are on your own, and feel like spoiling yourself.

1. Heat the butter in a frying pan until it is bubbling. Add the steak and cook for about 3 minutes on each side (medium done).
2. Season the steak during cooking with salt and pepper.
3. Meanwhile, heat sufficient oil in a second pan to give a depth of about 5 mm (¼ inch).
4. Add the 2 slices of bread, turning them over in the hot oil. Cook steadily until the underside is golden.
5. Turn the slices of fried bread over, making room for the egg. Carefully crack the egg into the pan.
6. Fry steadily for 2-3 minutes until the egg is just set – if the bread starts to brown too much, remove it from the pan and keep warm, draining on paper towels.
7. Spread one slice of fried bread quite generously with mustard. Top with the steak, some of the pan juices, the fried egg and finally the second slice of fried bread.
8. Garnish with watercress and serve immediately.

FROM THE TOP: Burger brunch; Hot dog toasties; Steak and fried egg toast

ALL WRAPPED UP

INDIVIDUAL BOEUF EN CROÛTE

4 fillet steaks, about 150 g (5 oz) each
150 ml (¼ pint) red wine
salt
freshly ground black pepper
1 garlic clove, peeled and crushed
50 g (2 oz) butter
75 g (3 oz) button mushrooms, sliced
400 g (14 oz) prepared puff pastry
75 g (3 oz) smooth pâté, cut into 4 slices
1 egg, beaten

Preparation time: 30 minutes, plus marinating overnight
Cooking time: 30 minutes
Oven: 200°C, 400°F, Gas Mark 6

1. Put the fillets steaks in a shallow dish. Add the wine, salt and pepper to taste, and the garlic.
2. Cover the dish and marinate the steaks in the refrigerator overnight.
3. Drain the steaks thoroughly on paper towels.
4. Melt the butter in a shallow pan, add the steaks and cook quickly for 1 minute on each side, just to seal them.
5. Remove the steaks from the pan and allow to cool.
6. Add the mushrooms to the fat remaining in the pan and cook for 2-3 minutes. Drain the mushrooms.
7. Roll out the puff pastry thinly and cut 4 rectangles, large enough to enclose the steaks.
8. Put a cooled steak in the centre of each pastry rectangle. Top with a quarter of the mushrooms and a thin slice of pâté.
9. Brush the pastry edges with beaten egg. Wrap the pastry round the steak and tuck the ends under, like a parcel. Pinch the edges, to seal.
10. Place on a greased baking sheet and brush all over with beaten egg to glaze.
11. Roll out the pastry trimmings and cut small leaves to decorate each 'parcel'. Fix in position and brush with beaten egg.
12. Place in a preheated oven and bake for about 25 minutes until the pastry is risen and golden.
13. The individual boeuf en croûte are equally good served hot or cold.

SPAGHETTI AL CARTOCCIO

275 g (10 oz) spaghetti
salt
2 tablespoons melted butter
4-5 tablespoons double cream
100 g (4 oz) peeled prawns
100 g (4 oz) cooked, shelled mussels
75 g (3 oz) smoked salmon trimmings, chopped
3 anchovy fillets, finely chopped
1 garlic clove, peeled and crushed
50 g (2 oz) grated Parmesan cheese
freshly ground black pepper

Preparation time: 15 minutes
Cooking time: about 20 minutes
Oven: 200°C, 400°F, Gas Mark 6

This pasta dish can be served either as a starter or as a light main course with salad.

1. Place the spaghetti in a pan of rapidly boiling salted water and cook for about 10 minutes until 'al dente' – just tender.
2. Meanwhile prepare the sauce: mix the melted butter with the cream, prawns, mussels, salmon, anchovies, garlic, Parmesan and pepper.
3. Lay 2 large sheets of greaseproof paper one on top of the other. Brush the top one generously with melted butter. Pull up the paper edges, creasing them, to make a well in the centre of the paper.
4. Drain the cooked spaghetti thoroughly and stir in the prepared seafood sauce.
5. Put the spaghetti and sauce into the well of the greaseproof paper. Pull the paper edges up and over loosely, and secure with paper clips or staples.
6. Put on a baking sheet. Place in a preheated oven and cook for 10 minutes until the paper puffs and crisps.
7. Remove from the oven, take to the table, and carefully slit the greaseproof paper to release the wonderful aroma.

FROM THE FRONT: Individual boeuf en croûte; Spaghetti al cartoccio

KIDNEY AND RICE KOULABIAC

40 g (1½ oz) butter
1 medium onion, peeled and finely chopped
225 g (8 oz) lamb's kidneys, skinned, cored and chopped
1 garlic clove, peeled and crushed
5 tablespoons cooked rice
salt
freshly ground black pepper
2 tablespoons sherry
2 tablespoons double cream
2 tablespoons chopped fresh parsley
1 hard-boiled egg, finely chopped
275 g (10 oz) prepared puff pastry
1 egg, beaten
Egg sauce:
2 hard-boiled eggs
1 teaspoon French mustard
juice of ½ lemon
150 ml (¼ pint) olive oil
1 tablespoon chopped fresh chives

Preparation time: 30 minutes, plus chilling
Cooking time: 40-45 minutes
Oven: 220°C, 425°F, Gas Mark 7

1. Melt the butter in a pan, add the onion and fry for 2-3 minutes.
2. Add the chopped kidneys and fry gently for 4-5 minutes.
3. Add the garlic, cooked rice, salt and pepper to taste, sherry and cream. Stir over the heat for 1 minute.
4. Add the parsley and chopped hard-boiled egg. Allow the mixture to cool.
5. Roll out the pastry to a 30 cm (12 inch) square.
6. Put the rice and kidney mixture into the centre.
7. Brush the pastry edges with beaten egg. Fold the corners of the pastry to the centre. Pinch the pastry edges together to seal, completely enclosing the filling.
8. Place on a greased baking sheet and chill for 20 minutes.
9. Brush all over with beaten egg to glaze. Place in a preheated oven and bake for 30-35 minutes.
10. For the sauce, separate the hard-boiled eggs. Sieve the yolks and chop the whites finely. Mix the sieved yolks with the French mustard and lemon juice. Beat in the olive oil gradually, and add salt and pepper to taste. Stir in the chopped egg white and chopped chives.
11. Serve the sauce with the hot koulabiac.

STILTON PANCAKES

4 large pancakes
melted butter, for brushing
300 ml (½ pint) thick white sauce
175 g (6 oz) Stilton cheese, crumbled
50 g (2 oz) walnuts, chopped
salt
freshly ground black pepper
1 bunch of watercress, washed, trimmed and finely chopped

Preparation time: 20 minutes
Cooking time: 20 minutes
Oven: 190°C, 375°F, Gas Mark 5

The pancakes do not need to be hot and freshly made, so this is a perfect dish for using ready-made bought pancakes or those that you have prepared in advance and frozen.

1. Brush the pancakes on one side with melted butter.
2. Brush 4 rectangles of greaseproof paper, each about 30 × 20 cm (12 × 8 inches), with melted butter.
3. Mix together the white sauce, Stilton, walnuts, salt and pepper to taste, and watercress.
4. Divide the Stilton filling between the pancakes, and roll each one up.
5. Place a rolled pancake in the centre of each rectangle of buttered greaseproof paper. Brush the pancakes with a little extra melted butter.
6. Fold the edges of the greaseproof neatly but loosely over each pancake, and secure either with staples or paper clips.
7. Put the pancake parcels on a large baking sheet.
8. Place in a preheated oven and bake for 20 minutes.

Preparing the Koulabiac
Kidneys can be fiddly to prepare and you will find it easier to remove the cores if you use kitchen scissors rather than a knife. Make sure that the filling is quite cold before you put it on the pastry; any warmth will cause the pastry to 'weep', and you will not get such a good finished result. Make sure too that you chill the assembled Koulabiac for the full 20 minutes. It is very important to pinch the pastry edges together very securely, otherwise the filling will spill out during baking. If the surface of the pastry 'crazes' during cooking, you can always give it an extra glaze with beaten egg, which will fill up any small cracks in the pastry. Any Koulabiac left over is delicious served cold, with a green salad.

TOP: Stilton pancakes. BOTTOM: Kidney and rice koulabiac

BANGERS AND BEANS IN AN OVERCOAT

1 tablespoon oil
4 plump sausages
350 g (12 oz) prepared puff pastry
1 egg, beaten
1 × 425 g (15 oz) can baked beans in tomato sauce
salt
freshly ground black pepper
2 tablespoons grated Parmesan cheese

Preparation time: about 20 minutes
Cooking time: about 25 minutes
Oven: 200°C, 400°F, Gas Mark 6

1. Heat the oil in a pan, add the sausages and fry gently for 3-4 minutes, turning them from time to time. Then remove and drain on paper towels.
2. Roll out the puff pastry quite thinly and cut 4 circles, each about 15 cm (6 inches) in diameter.
3. Brush the edges of the pastry circles with the beaten egg.
4. Lay a part-cooked sausage on each pastry circle and add a generous tablespoon of beans. Sprinkle with salt and pepper. Fold one half of each pastry circle over the sausage and beans and pinch the pastry edges together to seal.
5. Place on a greased baking sheet and brush with beaten egg to glaze. Sprinkle with Parmesan cheese.
6. Place in a preheated oven and bake for about 20 minutes.

GARLIC CHICKEN IN CABBAGE LEAVES

50 g (2 oz) butter, softened
3 tablespoons chopped fresh parsley
2 large garlic cloves, peeled and crushed
salt
freshly ground black pepper
4 chicken drumsticks, boned
8 large cabbage leaves
150 ml (¼ pint) white wine

Preparation time: 25 minutes, plus chilling
Cooking time: about 50 minutes
Oven: 180°C, 350°F, Gas Mark 4

Ask your butcher to bone the chicken drumsticks for you – it makes the preparation of the dish much less fiddly.

1. Mix the butter with 2 tablespoons of the parsley, the crushed garlic, and salt and pepper to taste.
2. Press a portion of the flavoured butter into the cavity of each boned drumstick. Wrap in cling film and chill for 1 hour – this firms up the butter filling.
3. Cut away the tough stalk from each cabbage leaf. Place in boiling water and blanch for 1 minute, then plunge into a bowl of cold water.
4. Drain the cabbage leaves on paper towels.
5. Wrap each chilled chicken drumstick in 2 cabbage leaves. Place in a shallow ovenproof dish.
6. Pour the wine over the cabbage parcels. Add salt and pepper and the remaining parsley.
7. Cover the dish with foil. Place in a preheated oven and cook for 50 minutes (check that the wine does not evaporate completely, adding a little extra wine or chicken stock if necessary during cooking).
8. Uncover the dish and serve immediately.

DUCK WITH APRICOT AND CHERRY SAUCE

4 duck portions, about 275-350 g (10-12 oz) each
oil, for coating
salt
freshly ground black pepper
1 × 200 g (7 oz) can apricot halves in natural juice
1 × 425 g (15 oz) can black cherries, drained

Preparation time: 20 minutes
Cooking time: 1-1½ hours
Oven: 200°C, 400°F, Gas Mark 6

1. Prick the duck portions at regular intervals with a fine skewer.
2. Rub the duck portions with oil and sprinkle with salt and pepper.
3. Put the duck on a wire tray over a roasting tin.
4. Place in a preheated oven and cook for 40 minutes. Allow the duck to cool slightly.
5. Put the apricot halves and their juice into the liquidizer and blend until smooth.
6. Stir the drained black cherries into the apricot purée.
7. Place each duck portion in the centre of a square of foil large enough to completely enclose it, shiny side uppermost. Pull up the foil edges.
8. Spoon over the fruit sauce. Pinch the foil edges together to seal.
9. Place the foil packets in the oven for a further 20-25 minutes. Open one parcel and test that the duck is tender. The overall cooking time will depend to a certain extent on the size of the duck portions.

BAKED PORK AND RED CABBAGE PARCELS

4 pork chops, trimmed
4 tablespoons apple sauce
1 tablespoon chopped fresh sage or 1 teaspoon dried
salt
freshly ground black pepper
8 large red cabbage leaves
200 ml (⅓ pint) cider

Preparation time: 15 minutes
Cooking time: about 1 hour 10 minutes
Oven: 180°C, 350°F, Gas Mark 4

1. Place the pork chops on the rack of the grill pan. Place under a preheated grill and cook for 3 minutes on each side. Cool slightly.
2. Spread 1 side of each pork chop with apple sauce. Sprinkle with sage and salt and pepper.
3. Cut away any tough stalk from the red cabbage leaves. Place in boiling water and blanch for 2 minutes, then plunge into a bowl of cold water.
4. Drain the cabbage leaves on paper towels.
5. Wrap each pork chop in 2 red cabbage leaves. Place in a shallow ovenproof dish.
6. Pour over the cider. Cover the dish with foil. Place in a preheated oven and cook for 1 hour.

FROM THE FRONT: Duck with apricot and cherry sauce; Garlic chicken in cabbage leaves

MUSTARD BAKED HERRINGS

4 herrings, headed and gutted
oil, for greasing
40 g (1½ oz) butter
1 small onion, peeled and finely chopped
1 garlic clove, peeled and crushed
25 g (1 oz) flour
150 ml (¼ pint) milk
150 ml (¼ pint) chicken stock
1 tablespoon horseradish mustard
salt
freshly ground black pepper

Preparation time: 10-15 minutes
Cooking time: 45-50 minutes
Oven: 190°C, 375°F, Gas Mark 5

LEFT: Mustard baked herrings. RIGHT: Plaice and spinach parcels

1. The herrings keep a better shape if unboned, but you may remove the bones if preferred.
2. Brush 4 rectangular pieces of foil, large enough to completely enclose each herring, with oil. Pull up the foil edges and lay a prepared herring along the centre of each one.
3. For the sauce, melt the butter, add the onion and fry gently for 3 minutes. Add the garlic. Stir in the flour and cook for 1 minute.
4. Gradually stir in the milk and chicken stock.
5. Bring to the boil, stirring, and add the mustard and salt and pepper to taste. Simmer the sauce for 5 minutes.
6. Spoon the sauce carefully over each herring.
7. Pull the edges of the foil up and over the herrings, pinching them together to seal. Place the foil parcels on a baking sheet.
8. Place in a preheated oven and cook for 35-40 minutes.

Variation:
Small mackerel can be used in place of the herring.

STUFFED SAVOURY ONIONS

4 large onions, peeled
25 g (1 oz) butter
6 rashers back bacon, chopped
3 tablespoons chopped fresh parsley
4 tablespoons fresh white breadcrumbs
2 eggs, beaten separately
2 tablespoons grated cheese
salt
freshly ground black pepper
450 g (1 lb) prepared shortcrust pastry
1 egg, beaten

Preparation time: 25 minutes
Cooking time: 50 minutes
Oven: 190°C, 375°F, Gas Mark 5

1. Carefully hollow out the onions, using a grapefruit knife, leaving 'shells' about 1 cm (½ inch) thick.
2. Place the onion shells in a pan of boiling water and par-boil for 6 minutes.
3. Chop the hollowed centres from the onions finely.
4. Melt the butter in a pan, add the chopped onion and bacon and fry gently for 3 minutes.
5. Mix the fried onion and bacon with the parsley, breadcrumbs, 1 beaten egg, cheese, and salt and pepper to taste.
6. Press the stuffing mixture well into each hollowed onion.
7. Roll out the pastry and cut 4 circles, each 18 cm (7 inches) in diameter.
8. Brush the edges of the pastry circles with the beaten egg.
9. Place a stuffed onion in the centre of each pastry circle. Pull up the pastry edges around the onion, pinching them together to seal.
10. Place the onions on a greased baking sheet and brush with beaten egg to glaze.
11. Roll out the pastry trimmings and cut some small leaves to decorate. Fix in position and brush with beaten egg.
12. Place in a preheated oven and bake for 40 minutes. Serve with a simple tomato or mushroom sauce.

PLAICE AND SPINACH PARCELS

4 large plaice fillets, skinned
12 anchovy fillets
freshly ground black pepper
2 tablespoons chopped fresh parsley
grated rind of ½ lemon
12 medium fresh spinach leaves
75 g (3 oz) butter, melted
Lemon sauce:
150 ml (¼ pint) mayonnaise
3 tablespoons double cream
grated rind of 1 lemon

Preparation time: about 15 minutes, plus chilling
Cooking time: about 45 minutes
Oven: 180°C, 350°F, Gas Mark 4

1. Check that there are no bones left in the plaice fillets. Lay them out flat.
2. Lay 3 anchovy fillets on each plaice fillet. Sprinkle with pepper, the parsley and lemon rind.
3. Roll up the plaice fillets. Secure with wooden cocktail sticks and chill for 30 minutes.
4. Place the spinach leaves in boiling water and blanch for 30 seconds. Drain on paper towels and lay them out flat.

5. Remove the cocktail sticks from each plaice fillet and roll each one up in 3 spinach leaves.
6. Put the plaice and spinach rolls into a greased shallow ovenproof dish. Spoon over the melted butter.
7. Cover the dish. Place in a preheated oven and cook for 40 minutes.
8. Meanwhile prepare the sauce. Put the mayonnaise, double cream, lemon rind and pepper to taste into a bowl. Stand the bowl over a pan of gently simmering water, stirring the sauce until it is heated through. Serve separately with the cooked fish.

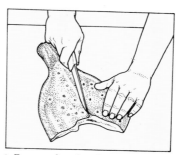

1. Remove head and cut down backbone with a sharp knife.

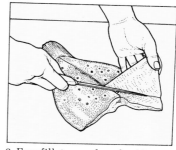

2. Ease fillet away from backbone.

LAMB EN CROÛTE

Serves 6
75 g (3 oz) butter
grated rind of 1 lemon
1 large garlic clove, peeled and crushed
1 tablespoon chopped fresh parsley
salt
freshly ground black pepper
6 large lamb cutlets
450 g (1 lb) prepared shortcrust pastry
beaten egg, for brushing

Preparation time: 25 minutes, plus chilling
Cooking time: 35-40 minutes
Oven: 190°C, 375°F, Gas Mark 5

If you don't like lamb slightly pink inside, then grill the cutlets lightly on each side and leave to cool, before coating in pastry.

1. Soften the butter. Mix with the lemon rind, garlic, parsley, and salt and pepper to taste.
2. Roll up the flavoured butter in a sausage shape, about the diameter of a ten pence piece, in a piece of greaseproof paper. Chill until firm.
3. Season the cutlets with salt and pepper.
4. Roll out the pastry fairly thinly and cut 6 rectangles, each large enough to enclose a cutlet.
5. Cut the butter into 6 slices and place one in the centre of each piece of pastry.
6. Place a cutlet on top and wrap the pastry over the cutlet, so that it is completely enclosed. Trim off the excess pastry and pinch the edges to seal.
7. Place on to a greased baking sheet and brush with beaten egg. Decorate with small shapes cut from pastry trimmings, if liked.
8. Bake in the oven for 35-40 minutes.
9. Serve hot with green vegetables, or cold with salad for a picnic.

STRUDEL PARCELS

1 large sheet of strudel paste
1 large cooking apple, peeled, cored and thinly sliced
juice and grated rind of 1 lemon
75 g (3 oz) dried apricots, chopped
75 g (3 oz) raisins
50 g (2 oz) demerara sugar
½ teaspoon ground mixed spice
melted butter, for brushing
icing sugar, for dusting

Preparation time: about 15 minutes
Cooking time: about 20 minutes
Oven: 200°C, 400°F, Gas Mark 6

Although strudel paste can be made at home, it is both time-consuming and fiddly. A very good ready-made strudel paste can be bought from most good delicatessens. If you find it difficult to buy, make 4 large thin pancakes, cooking them on one side only – put the filling on to the cooked side of the pancake, and fold up as below. Brush well with melted butter and bake for only 8 minutes. The filling will be slightly firmer.

1. Cut the sheet of strudel paste into 4 even-sized rectangles.
2. Mix the apple slices with the lemon juice and rind, dried apricots, raisins, demerara sugar and mixed spice.
3. Brush the pieces of strudel paste with melted butter.
4. Divide the apple filling between the 4 pieces of strudel paste, and fold up envelope fashion. Place seam side down on a greased baking sheet and brush with more melted butter.
5. Place in a preheated oven and bake for about 20 minutes.
6. Dust with sifted icing sugar and serve immediately.

HOT FRUIT SALAD

1 large firm banana, peeled and cut into 4 chunks
2 eating apples, cored and cut into thick wedges
1 large firm pear, peeled, cored and cut into wedges
4 greengages, stoned, or 12 ripe gooseberries
4 small plums, stoned
juice of 1 lemon
50 g (2 oz) butter
50 g (2 oz) soft brown sugar
2 tablespoons sherry
¼ teaspoon ground mixed spice

Preparation time: about 10 minutes
Cooking time: about 23 minutes
Oven: 190°C, 375°F, Gas Mark 5

1. Toss the banana, apples, pear, greengages and plums in the lemon juice.
2. Cut four 20 cm (8 inch) squares of foil and divide the fruit amongst them. Pull up the edges to make the foil cup shaped.
3. Put the butter, brown sugar, sherry and spice into a pan and stir over a gentle heat until dissolved.
4. Spoon the mixture evenly over the fruit.
5. Pull the foil edges up and over the fruit, pinching them together to seal.
6. Put the foil parcels on a baking sheet. Place in a preheated oven and cook for about 20 minutes.
7. Serve hot with cream or ice cream.

FROM THE LEFT: Hot fruit salad; Pear dumplings; Marzipan peaches

MARZIPAN PEACHES

50 g (2 oz) macaroons or ratafias, crumbled
juice and grated rind of 1 orange
4 good size peaches, halved and stoned
cornflour, for dusting
350 g (12 oz) marzipan
1 egg white, lightly beaten
caster sugar, for sprinkling
4 small bay leaves, to decorate

Preparation time: 25 minutes, plus standing
Cooking time: 15 minutes
Oven: 190°C, 375°F, Gas Mark 5

1. Mix the crumbled macaroons with the orange juice. Leave to stand for 20 minutes.
2. Sandwich the peach halves back together again with the macaroon mixture.
3. Roll each peach lightly in cornflour.
4. Roll out the marzipan quite thinly on a work surface dusted with cornflour. Cut 4 circles, each about 15 cm (6 inches) in diameter.
5. Stand a peach in the centre of each circle of marzipan. Pull up the edges of the marzipan, pinching them together to completely enclose the peach.
6. Place the marzipan peaches on a lightly greased baking sheet. Brush with beaten egg white and sprinkle with caster sugar and orange rind.
8. Place in a preheated oven and cook for about 15 minutes. Serve warm with cream, decorating each peach with a bay leaf.

This unusual recipe is well worth the careful preparation and cooking required to ensure an attractive appearance. It would make an impressive finale to a dinner party.

Choose peaches that are just ripe enough to cut in half, but not fully ripe; if the peaches are very soft when you start, the cooked result will be very 'squashy'. Make sure that the marzipan is really pliable before you start to mould it around the sandwiched peaches – it needs to be quite 'elastic' so that the marzipan does not crack, and so that it seals tightly where you pinch it together around the peaches. Glaze evenly with beaten egg white so that the baked marzipan-covered peaches have an all-over golden crust. You may find it easier to roll the brushed marzipan peaches in a mixture of the sugar and grated orange rind, rather than sprinkling them. For a quite different coating, the peaches could be rolled in finely chopped nuts prior to baking; blanched almonds would be the most suitable to use.

PEAR DUMPLINGS

4 large pears, peeled
juice of 1 lemon
450 g (1 lb) prepared shortcrust pastry
1 egg, beaten
4 tablespoons cranberry sauce

Preparation time: 25 minutes
Cooking time: about 35 minutes
Oven: 190°C, 375°F, Gas Mark 5

1. Carefully remove the core from the base of each pear, so that the stalk end of each pear is left intact.
2. Brush the prepared pears all over with lemon juice to prevent discoloration.
3. Roll out the pastry fairly thinly and cut 4 circles, about 20 cm (8 inches) in diameter.
4. Brush the edges of the pastry circles with the beaten egg.
5. Fill the base of each pear with a tablespoonful of cranberry sauce.
6. Carefully place a pear in the centre of each pastry circle. Pull up the pastry edges around the pear, pinching them together at the stalk end.
7. Place the pastry-covered pears on a greased baking sheet and brush with beaten egg to glaze.
8. If liked, roll out the pastry trimmings and cut small leaves to decorate. Fix in position and brush with beaten egg.
9. Place in a preheated oven and bake for 35 minutes. Serve hot with cream.

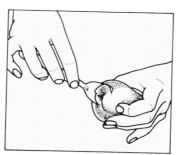 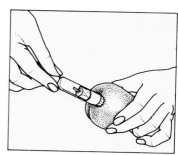

1. Coring with a teaspoon.   2. Coring with an apple corer.

FAMILY TREATS

PARTY LIGHTS

Serves 6
Ice cubes:
green food colouring
maraschino cherries
Drink:
1.2 litres (2 pints) lemonade
yellow food colouring

Preparation time: 15 minutes, plus chilling

Kids love bright colours, especially when it comes to drinks, and brightly coloured drinks can be made with very little effort. For extra effect, add contrasting coloured ice cubes.

1. For the ice cubes, measure the capacity of your ice cube tray by filling it with water and then tipping the water into a measuring jug.
2. Colour the water a deep green with food colouring.
3. Put a maraschino cherry into each compartment of the ice cube tray and fill up with the green water. Freeze until solid.
4. Mix the lemonade with sufficient food colouring to tint it a bright yellow.
5. Put 2-3 green cherry ice cubes into each glass and top up with the yellow lemonade.

PEANUT SANDWICH BALLS

Makes about 24
225 g (8 oz) full fat soft cheese
2 tablespoons peanut butter
75 g (3 oz) ham, finely chopped
3 tablespoons fresh brown breadcrumbs
100 g (4 oz) salted or dry roast peanuts, finely chopped

Preparation time: 20 minutes

1. Soften the cheese with the peanut butter in a bowl using a wooden spoon.
2. Beat in the chopped ham and brown breadcrumbs.
3. Form the mixture into about 24 small balls. Roll each one in chopped peanuts to give an even coating.
4. Spike the peanut sandwich balls on coloured cocktail sticks.

COCONUT FUNNY FACES

Makes about 12 sandwiched biscuits
75 g (3 oz) soft margarine
75 g (3 oz) caster sugar
3 egg yolks
½ teaspoon vanilla essence
100 g (4 oz) plain flour
50 g (2 oz) rice flour
75 g (3 oz) desiccated coconut
To decorate:
6-8 tablespoons lemon curd
4 tablespoons desiccated or long shred coconut
1 tablespoon cocoa powder
12 glacé cherries
12 small jelly sweets
angelica

Preparation time: 40 minutes, plus chilling
Cooking time: 12-15 minutes
Oven: 180°C, 350°F, Gas Mark 4

These biscuits can be guaranteed to put a smile on anyone's face, including grandma.

1. Cream the margarine and sugar together in a bowl until light and fluffy. Beat in the egg yolks and vanilla essence.
2. Fold in the sifted flours and coconut and work to a smooth dough. Chill for 30 minutes.
3. Roll out the biscuit dough very thinly and stamp out 24 circles using a 7.5 cm (3 inch) pastry cutter.
4. Put on to greased baking sheets. Place in a pre-heated oven and bake for 12-15 minutes until pale golden. Cool on a wire tray.
5. Sandwich the biscuits together in pairs with lemon curd.
6. Mix the desiccated coconut with the sifted cocoa powder.
7. Spread a little lemon curd on the top edge of each sandwiched biscuit and sprinkle with a little of the brown coconut, to look like hair.
8. Cut the glacé cherries in half and fix 2 on to each biscuit with small dabs of lemon curd for the eyes.
9. Add a jelly sweet nose and a mouth, cut from angelica, to complete the funny faces.

FROM THE FRONT: Peanut sandwich balls; Party lights; Coconut funny faces

FLYING SAUCERS

350 g (12 oz) prepared shortcrust pastry
225 g (8 oz) cooked meat, chopped (ham, chicken, beef, etc)
100 g (4 oz) cheese, grated
50 g (2 oz) salted peanuts, chopped
3 tablespoons tomato ketchup
freshly ground black pepper
beaten egg, to glaze

Preparation time: 20-25 minutes
Cooking time: 30-35 minutes
Oven: 190°C, 375°F, Gas Mark 5

1. Roll out the pastry thinly and cut out 8 circles, about 13 cm (5 inches) in diameter, to fit the saucer or scallop shell.
2. Line 4 saucers or shells with half the pastry.
3. Mix the chopped cooked meat with the cheese, peanuts, ketchup and pepper to taste.
4. Divide the filling amongst the pastry-lined saucers. Brush the pastry edges with beaten egg.
5. Lay the remaining pastry circles over the filling. Pinch the edges together to seal.
6. Glaze the top surface of the pastry with beaten egg.
7. Put the saucers or shells on a baking sheet and place in a preheated oven and bake for 30-35 minutes until golden brown. Serve either hot or cold.

CHEESY TWIST RINGS

Makes 24
100 g (4 oz) prepared puff pastry
1 egg, beaten
50 g (2 oz) cheese, finely grated
2 tablespoons sesame seeds

Preparation time: about 30 minutes, plus chilling
Cooking time: 12 minutes
Oven: 220°C, 425°F, Gas Mark 7

1. Roll out the pastry thinly and trim to a 30 cm (12 inch) square.
2. Cut the pastry in half into 2 even-sized rectangles, 30 × 15 cm (12 × 6 inches).
3. Brush one rectangle of pastry with beaten egg and sprinkle with the grated cheese.
4. Top with the second rectangle of pastry. Roll lightly to press the two pieces of pastry together.
5. Brush the top surface of the pastry 'sandwich' lightly with beaten egg and sprinkle with the sesame seeds.
6. Cut into thin strips, 15 × 1 cm (6 × ½ inch) wide.
7. Twist each strip 2 or 3 times, bringing the ends together in a circle. Pinch to seal. Place on a dampened baking sheet and chill for 30 minutes.
8. Place in a preheated oven and bake for about 12 minutes.

MARBLED EGGS

Makes 6
6 eggs
food colouring (see method)

Preparation time: 3 minutes, plus cooling
Cooking time: 10 minutes

These pretty mottled eggs are very simple to make, and they are a fun addition to a packed school lunch or picnic. Do not be mean with the food colouring – the more you add, the deeper the marbling.

1. Put the eggs into a pan and add sufficient cold water to completely cover them.
2. Bring the water to the boil and simmer the eggs steadily for 3 minutes. Remove the eggs carefully with a slotted spoon.
3. Add sufficient food colouring to the cooking water to tint it quite a deep colour – about 2 teaspoons.
4. Tap the eggs all over with the back of a spoon so that the shells craze.
5. Return the eggs to the coloured water and continue simmering for a further 7 minutes.
6. Plunge the eggs into a bowl of iced water to which you have added an extra teaspoon or two of the appropriate food colouring.

TUB O'BEANS

Serves 8
8 large round crisp bread rolls
oil, for brushing
1 × 425 g (15 oz) can baked beans
1 × 300 g (11 oz) can sweetcorn kernels, drained
4 large frankfurters, chopped

Preparation time: 15 minutes
Cooking time: 20 minutes
Oven: 190°C, 375°F, Gas Mark 5

1. Cut a thin slice from the top of each bread roll. Carefully hollow out most of the centre crumb, leaving shells about 1 cm (½ inch) thick. (You can keep the spare bread to make breadcrumbs.)
2. Brush the inside of the hollowed bread rolls with oil.
3. Put the rolls on to a baking sheet. Place in a preheated oven and bake for 10 minutes, until brown and crisp.
4. Meanwhile, heat the beans, sweetcorn and frankfurters in a pan.
5. Spoon the bean mixture into each hollowed bread roll and wrap each one in foil.
6. Return to the oven and bake for a further 10 minutes. Serve warm, with teaspoons for easy eating.

BANANA POPS

Makes 12

6 large firm bananas, peeled
12 wooden skewers or thin lolly sticks
350 g (12 oz) plain or milk chocolate
coloured hundreds and thousands or chocolate vermicelli

Preparation time: about 25 minutes, plus freezing

The choc-ice with a difference! Let the children come up with their own ideas for decorating the Banana pops – a child's name piped in icing; a face made from small coloured sweets; or a number decoration to celebrate a birthday.

1. Cut each banana in half crossways.
2. Fix each half banana on to a wooden skewer so that the skewer runs at least 5 cm (2 inches) inside the banana.
3. Place the bananas on a piece of foil and put in the freezer or ice compartment of the refrigerator for 1 hour.
4. Break the chocolate into pieces. Put it into a bowl and stand it over a pan of almost boiling water. Stir until the chocolate has melted.
5. Taking one banana from the freezer at a time, hold it over the bowl and spoon the melted chocolate over the banana to give an even coating. If the bananas are really cold, the chocolate coating will start to set immediately.
6. As soon as each banana is evenly coated with chocolate, sprinkle it with hundreds and thousands or vermicelli, or any other decoration of your choice.
7. Once each banana has been coated with chocolate and decorated, lay it carefully on a sheet of lightly oiled greaseproof paper. (To ensure that the bananas have a really perfect appearance, push the sticks into a large block of green oasis – the sort used for flower arranging – once they have been coated.)
8. As soon as the chocolate coating has set on the bananas, and the decorations are firmly in place, wrap the banana pops lightly in foil or freezer wrap, and return to the freezer or ice compartment. Serve ice-cold straight from the freezer.

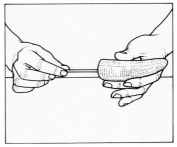

1. Pushing the skewer into the banana halves.

2. Coating the banana pop with chocolate.

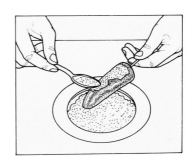

3. Spreading the decorations on the chocolate.

4. Pushing the completed banana pop into oasis.

ORANGE BANANA FLOATS

Serves 6
5 bananas, peeled
juice of 1 lemon
2 tablespoons clear honey
1.2 litres (2 pints) orange juice
6 scoops vanilla ice cream
6 thin slices orange (optional)

Preparation time: 10-15 minutes

This makes a delicious party drink for kids – serve it with spoons so that none of the ice cream is wasted at the bottom of the glass.

1. Chop the bananas and put into the liquidizer with the lemon juice and honey. Blend until smooth.
2. Add about half of the orange juice (depending on the size of your liquidizer), and blend once again until smooth.
3. Pour the orange and banana mixture into a large glass jug and stir in the remaining orange juice. Add a few ice cubes.
4. Put a scoop of ice cream into each of 6 tall tumblers. Pour over the orange and banana drink.
5. Make a small cut in each slice of orange, if using, and fix over the rim of each glass. Serve immediately with bendy straws and long handled spoons.

BUTTERFLY WINGS

Makes 24
3 egg yolks
50 g (2 oz) caster sugar
120 ml (4 fl oz) single cream
2 teaspoons vanilla essence
250 g (9 oz) plain flour
oil, for deep frying
icing sugar

Preparation time: 20-25 minutes
Cooking time: 3-4 minutes

1. Beat together the egg yolks, caster sugar, cream and vanilla essence in a bowl.
2. Add the flour and work to a smooth dough.
3. Roll out the dough quite thinly on a lightly floured board. Cut into 24 diamond shapes, using a wheel cutter.
4. Make a small cut in the centre of each pastry diamond – tuck the points of the diamond through the cut, and pull out slightly.

ANIMAL OPEN SANDWICHES

Makes 24 small sandwiches
6 large thin slices brown bread (taken from a standard large sliced loaf)
softened butter, for spreading
Marmite or meat paste, for spreading
2 small packets potato crisps

Preparation time: about 20 minutes

If you use the small animal shaped cutters, you should be able to get 4 open sandwiches from each slice of bread. There is no need to waste the trimmings from cutting out the shapes – blend the sandwich trimmings in the liquidizer until the texture of coarse crumbs. Mix with sufficient mayonnaise to bind. Divide into small balls about the size of a grape and roll in crushed crisps. If you don't have animal shapes, any other decorative shaped cutter can be used.

1. Spread the slices of bread with butter and then with a thin layer of Marmite or meat paste.
2. Crush the potato crisps fairly finely. The easiest way of doing this is to put the crisps on to a clean tea towel and to roll them gently with a rolling pin. Press the crushed crisps on to the Marmite or paste-covered bread slices.
3. Stamp out small animal shapes from the crisp-topped bread, using animal shaped cutters.

5. Fill a pan one third full of oil and heat to 190°C (375°F), or until a cube of bread browns in 30 seconds. Lower the shaped pastries into the hot oil, using a slotted spoon or spatula. Deep fry for 3-4 minutes until golden and crisp, then lift out carefully.
6. Drain the cooked pastries thoroughly on paper towels and dust with sifted icing sugar.

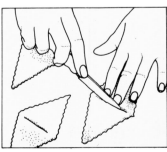 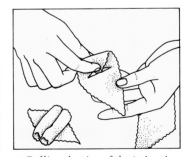

1. Cutting the slits in the diamond shapes.

2. Pulling the tips of the 'wings' through the slit.

FROM THE LEFT: Butterfly wings; Orange banana floats; Animal open sandwiches

REAL COFFEE SHORTBREAD

Makes 500 g (1¼ lb)
75 g (3 oz) ground almonds
175 g (6 oz) plain flour, sifted
175 g (6 oz) butter
75 g (3 oz) caster sugar
2 tablespoons finely ground fresh coffee

Preparation time: 20 minutes, plus chilling
Cooking time: 25-30 minutes
Oven: 160°C, 325°F, Gas Mark 3

Unlike traditional shortbread, this recipe makes a shortbread with a characteristic tang of fresh coffee.

1. Place all the ingredients in a mixing bowl and work together thoroughly with the fingertips until the mixture forms a smooth ball.
2. Chill the shortbread dough for 30 minutes.
3. Roll out the chilled dough on a lightly floured surface to about 1 cm (½ inch) thick.
4. Either cut into fingers or stamp out with shaped cutters – a diamond cutter makes a particularly pretty shape.
5. Place on to lightly greased baking sheets, allowing room for spreading. Chill for a further 30 minutes.
6. Place in a preheated oven and bake for 25-30 minutes until lightly golden. Allow to cool slightly before removing from the baking sheets.

NANAIMO BARS

Makes 16-20
100 g (4 oz) butter
50 g (2 oz) sugar
5 tablespoons cocoa powder
1 egg, beaten
1 teaspoon vanilla essence
75 g (3 oz) desiccated coconut
50 g (2 oz) chopped nuts
100 g (4 oz) digestive biscuits, crushed
Butter icing:
50 g (2 oz) butter
200 g (7 oz) icing sugar, sifted
1 egg
Chocolate topping:
175 g (6 oz) plain chocolate
15 g (½ oz) butter

Preparation time: 30 minutes, plus chilling
Cooking time: 3-4 minutes

CARROT COOKIES

Makes about 24
100 g (4 oz) butter
100 g (4 oz) caster sugar
1 egg, beaten
4 tablespoons coarse-cut marmalade
2 medium carrots, peeled and grated
200 g (7 oz) plain flour
½ teaspoon salt
½ teaspoon baking powder
finely grated rind of 1 orange
75 g (3 oz) raisins, chopped

Preparation time: about 20 minutes
Cooking time: 12-15 minutes
Oven: 180°C, 350°F, Gas Mark 4

1. Place the butter and sugar in a bowl and beat until soft and creamy. Add the beaten egg gradually.
2. Beat in the marmalade and grated carrots.
3. Sift the flour, salt and baking powder together and stir into the creamed mixture, together with the orange rind and raisins.
4. Place teaspoons of the mixture on to lightly greased baking sheets, allowing room for spreading.
5. Place in a preheated oven and bake for 12-15 minutes until lightly golden. Leave to cool on a wire tray.

1. Grease a tin about 23 cm (9 inches) square by 5 cm (2 inches) deep.
2. Put the butter and sugar into a pan and stir until the butter has melted.
3. Add the cocoa, beaten egg and vanilla essence. Stir over a gentle heat until the mixture thickens.
4. Remove from the heat and stir in the coconut, chopped nuts and crushed biscuits. Press into an even layer in the tin and chill.
5. For the Butter icing put the butter, icing sugar and egg into a bowl and beat until smooth and creamy.
6. Spread the Butter icing over the biscuit and coconut layer. Chill once again.
7. For the Chocolate topping, break the chocolate into pieces. Put into a bowl and stand it over a pan of almost boiling water. Stir until the chocolate has melted. Beat in the butter. Allow to cool.
8. Swirl the Chocolate topping over the Butter icing. Chill for 3-4 hours. Cut into squares for serving.

LEFT: Orange cup trifles. RIGHT: Nanaimo bars

ORANGE CUP TRIFLES

Serves 8

8 large oranges with good skins
4 trifle sponges
1 × 425 g (15 oz) can fruit (pear halves, apricots, etc)
1 packet jelly (any flavour)
300 ml (½ pint) double cream, whipped
crystallized orange and lemon segments, to decorate

Preparation time: 45-50 minutes, plus chilling

The orange cups can be filled with the sponge, fruit and jelly the day before, and then decorated with cream just before needed. Look for really big oranges, to make sure they will take all the filling.

1. Cut a thin slice from one end of each orange.

2. Carefully hollow out the centre flesh, using a grapefruit knife or spoon if possible. Chop the orange flesh, discarding any pips.

3. Chop the trifle sponges. Drain and chop the canned fruit, reserving the juice.

4. Divide the chopped orange flesh, sponge and canned fruit amongst the orange cups.

5. Chop the jelly into small pieces with kitchen scissors and put into a measuring jug. Add sufficient boiling water to make up to 300 ml (½ pint). Stir until dissolved.

6. Add the drained fruit juice and/or water to make up to just under 600 ml (1 pint).

7. Chill until the jelly is syrupy. Fill up each orange cup carefully with part-set jelly. Chill until the jelly has set completely.

8. Pipe whipped cream on top of each orange cup trifle and decorate with orange and lemon segments.

SHERRIED PRUNES

Makes about 1.25 kg (2½ lb)
1 kg (2 lb) large prunes
long strip of lemon peel
2 bay leaves
medium dry sherry (see below)

Preparation time: 5 minutes, plus 'topping up' and maturing

It is difficult to give an exact quantity of sherry, as the amount of sherry the prunes actually absorb depends greatly on the quality of the prunes. Prepare 2-3 months before you plan on giving them.

1. Put the prunes into 1 large- or 2 medium-sized kilner jars with the lemon peel and bay leaves.
2. Add sufficient sherry to well cover the prunes. Fit the lids on to the jars and leave to mature for 1 week.
3. Top up the jars with more sherry, to replace what has been absorbed.
4. Continue the 'topping up' process until the prunes have matured for 2 months.

CHOCOLATE BON BONS

Makes 20
20 maraschino cherries
225 g (8 oz) marzipan
225 g (8 oz) plain chocolate, melted

Preparation time: about 55 minutes, plus setting

These small chocolate and marzipan covered cherries make a wonderful gift for anyone with a sweet tooth.

1. Lay the maraschino cherries out on a piece of paper towel to absorb the excess maraschino syrup.
2. Divide the marzipan into 20 even-sized pieces and knead each one until smooth.
3. Carefully mould each piece of marzipan around a cherry, making sure that the cherries are completely enclosed.
4. Spike each marzipan covered cherry on to a fork and spoon over the melted chocolate, allowing the excess chocolate to drip off. Slide the cherries carefully on to a piece of lightly oiled greaseproof paper and leave until set.
5. Put a little melted chocolate into a small piping bag fitted with a writing nozzle, and pipe a swirl of chocolate on top of each bon bon. Leave until set.

SPICED APPLE BUTTER

Makes about 1.25 kg (2½ lb)
1 kg (2 lb) cooking apples, cut into small pieces
grated rind of 1 lemon
½ teaspoon ground mixed spice
½ teaspoon ground ginger
½ teaspoon ground mace
caster sugar (see method)

Preparation time: 15 minutes
Cooking time: 35 minutes

This fruit butter can be eaten with toast, but it also makes a delicious topping for ice cream.

1. Place the apples in a pan with the lemon rind and spices, and sufficient water to just cover. Simmer gently until the fruit is soft.
2. Push the apple pulp and its liquid through a sieve to give a smooth purée.
3. Weigh the apple purée and place in a clean pan, adding 350 g (12 oz) sugar to each 450 g (1 lb) fruit purée.
4. Stir over a gentle heat until the sugar has dissolved. Continue cooking gently until thick, smooth and creamy, stirring from time to time.
5. Pour into small warmed clean jars and cover with waxed discs. Top with screw-top lids or circles of greaseproof paper, secured with rubber bands.
6. Label when quite cold. Stored in a cool place, the apple butter will keep for 1 month.

ORANGE AND WALNUT FONDANTS

Makes about 500 g (1¼ lb)
450 g (1 lb) icing sugar, sifted
1 egg white, lightly beaten
2-3 tablespoons double cream
finely grated rind of 1 orange
orange food colouring
icing sugar, to dust
100 g (4 oz) walnuts, finely chopped
small walnut halves, to decorate

Preparation time: about 25 minutes, plus drying

Fondant sweets can be made from a cooked fondant mixture, but you then need to use a sugar thermometer. The following recipe is somewhat easier if you are a first-time sweetmaker.

1. Place the icing sugar in a bowl, add the egg white, cream and orange rind and mix together.
2. Knead to a smooth paste, adding a few drops of orange food colouring to tint the paste a pale orange.
3. Work the chopped walnuts into the fondant paste.
4. Dust your hands with icing sugar. Break the fondant off into small pieces about the size of a large cherry. Mould into neat oval shapes.
5. Place the shaped fondants on to a wire tray and press a walnut half into the top of each one.
6. Leave to dry out for about 8 hours or overnight.

FROM THE FRONT: Chocolate bonbons; Orange and walnut fondants; Sherried prunes

INDEX